SEVEN
STEPS
· TO ·
INNER
POWER

SEVEN STEPS · TO · INNER POWER

A MARTIAL ARTS MASTER REVEALS HER SECRETS FOR DYNAMIC LIVING

BY

GRANDMASTER

TAE YUN KIM

NEW WORLD LIBRARY
NOVATO, CALIFORNIA

New World Library
14 Pamaron Way
Novato, CA 94949

© 1991 Grandmaster Tae Yun Kim
Cover design: Principia Graphica
Text design: Nancy Benedict

Cover and chapter head photo:
Doug Petit, © 1991
All author photos: Scott H. Salton
Word Processing: Deborah Eaglebarger
Typography: G&S Typesetters, Inc.

Library of Congress Catalog Card Number
91-178213
First Printing, April 1991
Printed in the U.S.A. on acid-free paper
Distributed by Publishers Group West

10 9 8

Blade of grass fluttering in the wind
Breaking rock,
Within.

Contents

CONTENTS

CHAPTER THREE

Three Tools of the Jung SuWon Warrior   45

Preface

Consider your hand for a moment — the softness of the skin. Imagine the bones and ligaments within. As you flex your fingers, think of the dexterity of this part of you that you so often take for granted.

Can you imagine this hand going through a brick, breaking it to pieces? Can you imagine it going through a stack of ten bricks? Maybe you think this is an impossible accomplishment for yourself or for anyone.

I assure you it's not.

But you may argue that your hand is softer and less dense than a brick. Of course it is. But is it not your thought that propels your hand? Is it not your thought that moves you throughout your life?

What I can teach you will enable you to break not only bricks but also the harder barriers that may be blocking happiness and fulfillment in your life.

I can teach you to be a true martial arts warrior. You may at first think this means I will teach you to be aggressive or to be a bully. Not at all. Have you ever observed a blade of grass that grows through the cement or the small tree that grows on solid rock? Look carefully. It is the cement or the rock that cracks. We could say that the blade of grass and the small tree are being aggressive, which is true. But is it not more accurate to say that they are only being true to their own lives? They are being true warriors.

This, then, is the understanding of Jung SuWon, which

means: "the way of uniting body, mind, and spirit in total harmony."

But first, to understand the origins of what I teach, and why I teach, it may be helpful to relate some experiences that influenced my life. These events gave me an understanding of the knowledge I now want to share with you. This knowledge is practical and provable.

People and events can shape someone for good or bad. But you alone have power over these things, more power than you realize. It does not matter how bad circumstances may seem. What I discovered was that how I dealt with circumstances was much more important than the circumstances themselves. My earliest memories were of the Korean War. I was five years old, and I couldn't understand why explosions were everywhere, why people were trying to hurt me. I remember running day and night as my family fled the communist invasion. I couldn't understand why the world was suddenly crazy. I was only five. Why would anyone want to kill me? My playmate was a year older than I. I was so tired, but she kept encouraging me to keep moving, to keep running. She was a short distance from me, encouraging me again, when another explosion blew her apart.

I'm not likely to forget what I saw. It was one of those moments that was too terrible to seem real. To call that a bad experience would be an understatement. But even then, in the midst of the bad, was the formation in my mind of something uniquely good. It was at that moment that I unknowingly made a decision that would forever change my life: I wasn't going to run anymore. I didn't know why, or even how, but I believed there had to be a way to stand up to this.

Two years later I began to discover a way. It was a blue-gray morning in Kinchom Province when I was awakened by a shout. The war was two years past, but sudden sounds still had an unsettling effect. Cautiously sliding back a rice-paper window my uneasiness disappeared as I saw something that instantly captivated me. It was beautiful. There, in the early morning fog, I discovered my uncles practicing an ancient martial art. The mists swirled with their fluid kicks, their bodies glistened in the first light of dawn. It touched a deep and natural feeling inside me. Nothing in my mind seemed so mystical and yet natural. To my seven-year-old mind, this was worthwhile. More than worthwhile, it was exciting. It was important. Nothing seemed so perfect. I had to learn this art. Little did I know how it would affect my life.

Teaching martial arts to a child is not unusual; in fact, it is a common practice. However, when I asked my uncles to teach me, my desire was met with laughter. Being seven years old was not the obstacle. I had forgotten the obstacle that in my culture was insurmountable.

I had forgotten that I was a girl.

Girls did not learn the martial arts. I was told it is the place of women to learn to cook and sew. Why? Simply because for centuries it had always been that way. No, that was silly; they wouldn't teach me. I should look forward to growing up, getting married, and having twelve sons. But, somehow, to me that didn't make sense. The desire in my heart was constant, as was my persistent asking. Finally my uncles relented, confident that when I experienced the difficulty and bruises I would surely give up.

Every morning, every day, I practiced. The work was hard and the bruises were many. But, to my uncles' surprise, I didn't give up. To their further bewilderment, I progressed.

As I grew in my martial art, the difficulties I encountered were enormous. Difficulty not in the art itself, but in the resistance I encountered from people's belief that a woman couldn't do it and, furthermore, shouldn't be able to do it. I had to wear slacks to hide the bruises so the other children wouldn't laugh at me. My family was convinced there was surely something wrong with me. Proud of my accomplishments if I were a boy, they regarded me as one who had brought shame on them. Still, I felt I had to be true to something deeper within myself. I had a burning desire to be the best martial artist I could possibly be. But because my desire was controversial for oriental culture, I was simply dismissed as someone who was unbalanced.

However, a year later, at the age of eight, I discovered that not everyone thought I was crazy. A martial arts master recognized and acknowledged my desire by accepting me as his student. I was extremely fortunate, for this gifted master trained me in unusual and unique ways.

For many years I trained with him in the nearby mountains. There I learned things that opened my eyes to a world I never knew existed. Year upon year passed as I began to understand the deeper teachings and secrets of martial arts that would eventually define what I now teach today.

Jung SuWon is more than a martial art. It is not a sport. True, it includes a physical form, but my teaching goes far beyond hard martial art forms that are strictly of foot and fist. Jung SuWon includes spiritual principles and practices that can lay the foundation of your inner power and physical strength, and that can develop your whole being. Thus, its mental and spiritual aspects are not separate from its physical form, and never could be. This martial art is essentially the art of living life itself. And this is what I consider to be the true "way" of the martial arts warrior — not just overcoming in combat, but a complete overcoming in every aspect of our daily living. When you learn this art, there will be no obstacle you cannot overcome.

It is from my experiences that I've proved this fact. Others said it was impossible when I, a woman, attained a black belt in my martial art. Then (more impossible) I, still a woman, became a female Master. And then (absolutely impossible!) I became a female Grandmaster. Well, so much for what is supposedly impossible.

People may say of a journey that it's long and they'll not bother to start. Take one step on the longest journey and you've shortened it.

But journeys are not accomplished without a map. And it is for this reason that I'm writing this book.

The art of Jung SuWon never failed me in becoming one of the highest-ranked female martial artists in the world. It has not failed those I've taught. I've taught them to listen to an everpresent Consciousness deep within, whom I call the "Silent Master."

Like the fabric of a tapestry, one thread will always lead to many others. I never found myself stopping with one achievement or another. If this person or that person can do something, why not me? If I fail, I'll try again. And again. Has anything worthwhile ever been accomplished without effort? If something has never been done, why should that stop you? My life has been made up of accomplishments that many well-meaning people told me were impossible.

I've founded schools and spread my teaching wherever I've gone. The demand has been ever constant, and it is growing. Whether teaching corporate executive seminars or teaching students in one of my schools, I've found many people who share goals and needs that are not unique to me, but are universal to the desires of all people regardless of sex, race, or creed.

Learning Jung SuWon (uniting body, mind, and spirit) will bring incredible physical and mental power to your life. I offer you this book — the map and guide of this art that has served me so well.

Grandmaster Tae Yun Kim

CHAPTER 1

Your Silent Master

THE POWER OF YOUR TRUE SELF

THE QUESTION . . . WHO AM I?

This is a question that is unique to human consciousness, certainly fundamental, sometimes difficult, but absolutely essential if you wish to express your fullest potential in life. Suppose I were to tell you that you are aware of only a limited portion of yourself, that you may not have yet discovered your self, your *true* self, and that you have yet to touch upon an enormous creative power within you that can reshape your life completely.

Who am I?

A quick answer may bring this response: "I am an engineer." Or, "I am a person who likes people; I am full of stress and anxiety; I am a mother; I am a nobody; I am athletic; I am intellectual; I am shy . . ." Note how often we tend to describe ourselves with positive or negative personality characteristics that we've developed or acquired over the years and accepted as being "us." Most of us do not look much deeper than that.

So, ask "Who am I?" now. What do you want to become? Where are you today? What have you accomplished or failed to accomplish? Do you have the career you want, the relationships you want? Do you like who you are? Are you happy? Have you realized your dreams and goals?

The truth is, you are exactly where you are because of the way you answered "Who am I?" Why? Because how you answer the question determines what *choices* you make for yourself moment to moment every day of your life.

You choose only what you believe is possible to choose, and these choices determine what you do with your life and who you become. If you believe you are shy, for instance, you will not choose to be a performer, even if your talent and inner desire are obvious. If you believe you aren't a good student, you may not choose a course of study that could lead you to the job you'd really like. It is very important, then, to know the absolute truth about yourself and your capabilities.

The purpose of this book is to show you that you may have made limited choices based on limited information about yourself. So we are here together to ask the question, Who am I—*really*?

If you're satisfied with your life at this moment, the question may hold no interest for you right now. But if, on the other hand, you find yourself holding dreams that feel so true, yet somehow out of reach, if you feel unfulfilled, frustrated, alienated, empty, if you feel you haven't done what you want, if there is more that you desire, more that you want to accomplish, if you feel that even though your life is satisfactory in most respects you nevertheless have a yearning to realize a deeper sense of joy, peace, and purpose, it is time to extend your vision of who you are.

2

No matter who you are, no matter where you are, no matter what obstacles and limitations exist around you at this moment, you can change your life, your health, and your state of mind completely. You can decide who you want to become.

THE ANSWER . . . SIX SILENT MASTER IMAGES

Who are you? Waiting quietly within you is a Presence, a Force, a state of *Consciousness* that gives you power to overcome mental and physical limitations in your life, power to harmonize and change discordant situations, power to create and to achieve goals, power to experience peace and joy regardless of the circumstances around you—power to be who you really are.

In Jung SuWon, I call this Consciousness your *Silent Master*. When you find this Consciousness, your Silent Master within yourself, you take control of your life. Before, you may have been drifting through life; now you are driving through life. You experience a new freedom, peace of mind, creativity, and harmony that makes your life fulfilling, purposeful, joyous, and dynamic. You find yourself glad to be alive every day for the sheer pleasure of experiencing life, of experiencing yourself!

I teach the art of Jung SuWon to awaken you to this powerful Presence within, to enable you to recognize and bring forth your Silent Master.

Consider the following six statements about your Silent Master Consciousness, which I call Silent Master Images. I use the word "image" instead of "statement" deliberately. When you read the section on visualization you'll understand why. Because these Images form the basis of my Jung SuWon philosophy, they will be developed in detail throughout the book. For now, however, regard each as a seed-thought designed to blossom into practical understanding of your true being and power.

Six Silent Master Images

IMAGE I

You Are One of a Kind

Your Silent Master is your Real Self, your original Self. It expresses Itself through your thinking, through true Ideas and Thoughts in your mind. It is your eternal Selfhood that exists apart from your brain (which is a sensory processor only) and the personality traits imposed on you from your environment.

IMAGE II

YOU AND THE LIFE FORCE ARE ONE

*Your Silent Master Consciousness
was born out of the infinite
Life Force creating and animating
the Universe. You exist as a
part of the Universe; therefore,
It is the Life Force creating
and animating you. It is
the power that beats your heart.
Because you are this Consciousness,
whatever qualities the Life Force
possesses, you possess also.*

IMAGE III

Your Thoughts Create Reality

*Your Silent Master Consciousness
knows Itself to be immaterial in
substance, but It also takes form
(manifests) as your
physical body
and the material
world around you.
Thus, you may
describe yourself
as being
both immaterial (spiritual)
and material (physical) at
the same time.*

8

IMAGE IV

You Are Creative Energy

Your Silent Master knows Itself as the Source of mental, emotional, and material Energy—your Energy, which you are free to utilize and control in creating what you desire. Therefore, you are a Co-Creator, cooperating with the Life Force of the Universe to shape yourself and the world around you.

IMAGE V

You Have the Power to Fulfill Your Dreams

*Your Silent Master is
completely aware, infinitely
Intelligent, and ready to
give you all the insight,
information, and direction you
need to fulfill your dreams,
ambitions, and goals. In fact,
this Consciousness is the
Source of all your true desires.*

IMAGE VI

YOU ARE COMPLETE, PEACEFUL, AND FULFILLED

Your Silent Master expresses completeness, fulfillment, harmony, peace, joy, and love, and imparts these qualities to everything It creates.

These six images reflect the Consciousness that is within you now. How does your Silent Master express Itself? How does It create? With thoughts and ideas. You, expressing your Silent Master, will learn to create what you desire by thinking in a new way, by thinking Its thoughts. Then, as indicated before, these thoughts and ideas will take material form as your body and emotions, as events and things.

As soon as you contact and identify with this Silent Master within, you will necessarily begin to look at yourself and understand yourself differently. What you think to be your "self" may say, "I am a failure." But your Silent Master says, "I have mental and physical strength to act and achieve." Your limited self may say, "I am afraid." Your Silent Master says, "I have no fear because I am the Source of all real power." Your limited self may say, "I am sick, and there is nothing I can do." Your Silent Master says, "I am eternally well and whole, and I can prove it." Your limited self may say, "I doubt, and I give up." Your Silent Master says, "I know, and I persist until I demonstrate my Truth."

Much more will be said about the qualities of your Silent Master and the ways you can bring It forth, for this is the purpose of the Jung SuWon art set forth in this book. Translated from Korean, "Jung" means "mind," the part of you that is the thinker. "Su" means the corporeal forms, including you, that are created by the incorporeal Life Force of the Universe. "Won" means the balancing and harmonizing unity of all creation with this Life Force. Therefore, Jung SuWon is the art form that describes the way you, as an individual mind, reclaim your unity with the Life Force of the Universe. This unity, as we now know, is your Silent Master Consciousness, and your consciously achieving this unity is the goal in studying Jung SuWon. This unity is your birthright!

THE DISTRACTION . . .

First, however, it's important to ask why the Silent Master is so named. Why is it silent? If all this power and dominion is available, why isn't it automatically out there healing you and your problems, making you the strong, successful, achieving person you want to be? Where has the Silent Master been all these years?

The Silent Master has always been there. It is silent only when we are not aware of It, when we do not focus on It, when we do not identify It as our Real Self. It is silent out of neglect—our neglect. It takes effort to listen to that which is silent. But when you make the decision to find your Silent Master, Its power begins to unfold to just the degree you strive to open yourself to receive It. So the question is not, Where has the Silent Master been? The question is, Where have you been? Let us answer this question, because in so doing you will see better how to open up to a new conception of yourself.

Isn't it interesting that the name given to our beginning is "conception"? We were "conceived" by our parents. And truly, from the day we were born, we have been in the business of forming concepts about ourselves.

Perhaps one of the first concepts you formed was that you were dependent. All the care, nourishment, and visibility you received came from outside yourself, from your immediate environment, most likely first from your parents, and then from school, work, and social environments. Because of your dependency as a small child, the persons first responsible for your care began to shape your identity according to their beliefs and expectations. How? Primarily by telling you what was "good" and what was "bad." Many things they taught benefited you. As a young, dependent child, it was usually in your best interests to learn from the people who were taking care of you. Most often, they had your best interests at heart. But many things you took as fact were only opinions.

Some of your behaviors were biologically programmed. No one had to teach you to cry, to smile, to laugh, feel hunger and thirst, or pain and pleasure. But even these automatic behaviors were subject to the pressures of approval and disapproval by authority figures, so that possibly you soon learned to hide, avoid, or distort natural impulses, impulses that were designed to help you know yourself.

Because of your dependency in your formative years, the pressure to conform to group standards outside yourself, whether in the family, school, or society at large, was enormous. As a child you couldn't alienate the people who were responsible for your physical and emotional survival, so you went along with them the best you could. Perhaps you resisted certain concepts about yourself along the way, but for the most part, you accepted what others had to say about you. And you acted accordingly. Why shouldn't you? "They" probably had the best intentions. Conformity was meant to be a good thing, something that would allow you to adjust and get along with the world with minimum conflict.

As you continued to interact with your environment, you learned how to act to avoid conflict, to avoid the displeasure of authority figures, and to secure praise and pleasure. You may have learned that the path of least resistance was to do what was expected of you, do what you were told, not be too different, and not to argue with the system. Notice that although the system was designed to give you a share of safety and security, it did not guarantee happiness, or fulfillment, or freedom—or any of the things that make life truly worth living.

By the time you reach the point where you are ready to

depend only on yourself, you are not automatically free from those prior influences. The programming is usually set.

The person you are is the person "they" taught you to be.

Now many of the choices you make—even your most important choices such as a spouse or a career—are really "their" choices. Even some of your so-called good beliefs may not reflect your true being. For example, a person who has become a perfectly respectable lawyer may have been thwarted from expressing his true love of designing cars. When this happens, as it does to many people, you must recognize that you are simply being a "copy" of other peoples' expectations, and not your original self. You may have developed an entire personality and life that has little to do with your true self. This is like being the Biblical house built on sand. It must surely fall when it is stressed, one way or another. Certainly, this "copy" will never feel a sense of peace or fulfillment even if it manages to get by and even if it has all the material comforts of life.

THE SOLUTION . . .

But you can know yourself! Right now! Your Silent Master is your original self still waiting to be born. You can make the decision to begin replacing the false concepts about yourself with the knowledge of your true being. You can stop being a receiver only, and start being a giver.

You can stop being self-destructive, and become a creator. You can be who you want to become. That is why you're here, living now: to learn, to overcome, to grow into the fullness of your being, to find your power and your purpose, and to live it! The decision to seek your Silent Master means you're in school again. Now, your life is your classroom. You will use all the obstacles, negatives, and limitations in your life as opportunities to demonstrate your dominion. You and your Silent Master can work together, listen to each other, and grow until you realize you are One.

I call this the Way of the Jung SuWon Warrior. You *will* have to change, and sometimes newness can be frightening. When your eyes have adjusted to darkness for a long time, and someone suddenly draws the curtain back, does not the bright light of normal daylight cause you discomfort, even pain? Just so, in some ways your limited self may be living in comfortable darkness.

But the rewards of becoming new are great. If you are willing to experience and conquer initial discomfort, you will soon grow accustomed to the brightness and see a whole new world illumined by this light! And you will remember every step of the way that the obstacles and limitations you attack are destined to fall because they were never a part of your Real Self.

As you change, you will be opening up to new opportunities, new challenges! Does not the small fish that hatches upstream fare great risks in swimming to the much larger ocean where it will grow big and strong? Yet, isn't this risk preferable to remaining upstream and living a smaller self?

You will see that the Way of the Warrior is to realize who you are in Truth and to demonstrate it. You will see that the work of the Warrior is joyous, that your perseverance is rewarded with increasing faith in your Silent Master and in love for yourself and others, and that your victory is assured! Because you already *are* one with your Silent Master.

CHAPTER 2

Seeking Your Silent Master

TAPPING INTO YOUR POWER

You now may have an inkling of what your Silent Master is. You know something of how It will enable you to create and shape your life according to your original, unique self. But where do you start? How do you bring forth your Silent Master?

In your *thinking* right now.

The power of the Silent Master within you is the power of *right thinking*, and the difference between a limited you and an unlimited you begins with your attitude and state of mind. So, your first step in taking charge of your life is to learn to take charge of your thinking. In Jung SuWon, we do this through practicing five principles of mental conduct.

But first, what is so important about mental conduct? Just as we all obey physical rules of conduct in society so that we all function in an optimum manner, mental rules of conduct enable our creative minds to function in an optimum fashion.

Demonstrating the Law of Manifestation

Remember this Silent Master Image from the first chapter?

III

---

*Your Silent Master
Consciousness knows Itself to
be immaterial in substance,
but It also takes form
(manifests) as your physical
body and the material world
around you . . .*

Everything that has taken form in your life—your body, your home, your job, your relationships—began first as an immaterial *thought form*, which can be a specific visual image or simply a general attitude and feeling. When you look at everything you've manifested in your life now, you're looking at a picture of the quality of your thinking and feeling.

This relationship between your thinking and the world you create is a universal law of manifestation. The proof that it is a law lies in your demonstrating the law. That is, when you begin to see how your controlled thinking creates what you set out to create, you no longer doubt the validity of this law. In fact, even little demonstrations inspire you to greater levels of achievement. Later we'll talk more specifically about how to create greater good for yourself with your thinking, but in this chapter we are concerned with the preliminary steps that will prepare you to become a consciously creative thinker.

Everything external in life was first internal in thought, so no permanent change can come about merely by attempting to fix or rearrange external conditions. Yet, that's usually what we try to do. When we see the symptoms of something wrong in our lives, we usually try to get rid of the symptoms instead of getting rid of the mental condition that's *causing* the symptoms. Unfortunately, we tend to look only at the surface of most situations. Why? Because searching for the cause of a situation requires more insight than is obvious at first glance; it takes time and effort to search below surface appearances.

For example, a friend who shares my interest in gardening had an expensive plant that was dying. The leaves were turning yellow and dropping, so she spent considerable effort giving it more light, then more shade, then more plant food, then more water, then less water, and on and on. Frustrated, she brought the plant to me. I recognized that the symptoms had nothing to do with any surface problem, but were from bacteria attacking the roots. I had to pull the plant out of the soil to get at the real problem. To her amazement, when I uprooted the plant, cleaned it, and replanted it, the problem disappeared. What I proved to her was that the *cause* of any problem must be identified before we can treat the problem effectively.

We can see other examples of our tendency to treat symptoms rather than causes in our everyday lives. A person may divorce an unsatisfactory marriage partner, only to attract another person with the same unsatisfactory characteristics, or worse. Another person may have a cancer surgically removed completely, only to find that it grows back again. In both instances, the thinking (which includes attitudes and emotions as well as thoughts) that *caused* the condition was not changed; therefore, the external condition did not change.

But what happens? We most likely hear the first person declare, "You see, another failed relationship! It's like I told you, there are no good people left in this world. I have the worst luck in relationships. Even if there is somebody good for me out there, either they won't like me, or I'll never find them." We may hear the second person say, "You see! Cancer is an incurable, fatal disease. I may as well accept it and live as well as I can until it kills me."

In both examples, these persons are voicing the very limitation—and false information about themselves—that we are here to overcome. They are basing their statements on outward material evidence. They believe their statements are true because they don't realize they created the evidence with their own thinking! They don't realize that their statements are actually *excuses* for failing to challenge life and change themselves.

Yes, it takes a lot of work to challenge your beliefs, a lot of courage to ask yourself if you're making true statements about yourself or simply making excuses for being lazy or weak-minded and refusing to change yourself.

This brings us to the five principles of mental conduct that lay the groundwork for your most unlimited creative thinking. If you put these principles into practice, you will discover you have begun to eliminate the clouds of counterproductive thinking that obstruct your vision, which paves the way for you to begin consciously creating a new life.

FIVE PRINCIPLES OF MENTAL CONDUCT

1. Identify Your Fears and Weaknesses and Conquer Them

Don't Be Afraid of Your Weaknesses

Most of us have an innate desire to be "good" people. If you look around at your associates, you may find it difficult to find a person who says, "Yeah, I'm a mean, ornery, bad person, and I like myself that way." More likely what you'll find are people who, in spite of what faults they have, defend their self-image of being a good person, of being "right," and of deserving some respect. In fact, maybe this describes you.

That's to be expected because we all are a mixture of strengths and weaknesses. And most of us live life as though we're "on stage," performing roles of mother, father, bread-winner, employee, employer, student, and so on. As we perform, the strengths and weaknesses of our performances are constantly being evaluated, usually by ourselves, and certainly by others. We have certain qualities called "strengths" that tend to lead us into greater harmony and peace; and we have other qualities called "weaknesses" that tend to undermine or sabotage the good we try to do.

Because we are performance oriented, we have a natural tendency to show or emphasize our strengths, and gloss over or ignore our weaknesses. We do this for survival, we assume. It's part of "putting our best face forward," which we think gives us higher performance ratings. And we generally believe that higher performance ratings mean a better life. But do they really? Do we gain anything by assessing only one part of ourselves?

Again, ask yourself "Who am I?" To really put your best face forward, you must be willing to look as hard at your weaknesses as you do your strengths and say, "I am a mixture of both." Why? So you can eliminate the weaknesses. How? By looking carefully at yourself and getting to know yourself. Take a piece of paper and pencil and actually list your strengths and weaknesses. List ten of each. See how easy or difficult this task is. See how well you really know yourself. But bear in mind that you must be careful in assessing your strengths and weaknesses.

If you were given a bag filled with real and synthetic diamonds and told to separate the real ones, your first task would be to gain complete knowledge of the qualities of the real diamonds as well as the characteristics of the synthetic ones. As you went about this task you wouldn't impose emotional value judgments on either kind. You wouldn't say, "This wonderful, beautiful, real diamond goes in this pile," and "This disgusting, terrible, phony synthetic goes in that pile." No; it would be an objective, clinical undertaking designed only to create a group of real diamonds.

However, this objectivity may not always be so easy. When a surgeon operates on a patient, he cannot be fearful of the amount of blood or hesitate to use his knife and cut through tissue. His objective is to reach that malignancy or make the adjustment that will make his patient well again. Let's take this example one step further and imagine that you are not only the surgeon but also the patient. Of course it's scary. But you must have the courage to operate on yourself with the same objectivity to rid yourself of that which can harm you. And what is the result? You feel a sense of peace because now you are well and whole.

So, look clinically at your strengths and weaknesses. You don't need to make value judgments on yourself. When you find your strengths, decide to keep them, but do not become overly confident or egotistical. When you find your weaknesses, determine to eliminate them, but do not fall in a mire of depression, dejection, or self-condemnation.

How do you know when you have eliminated your weaknesses? When you are no longer dominated by them. For instance, if a former alcoholic refuses to drink, but is afraid to look at a bottle, to some extent she is still being held by the disease. When she can look at the bottle and say, "I am cured, and I am not afraid of you," she is no longer dominated by the disease. Just so, when you no longer fear you'll fall prey to your weaknesses, you feel your true strength.

Releasing Weaknesses Releases Your Energy

The process of taking a hard look at yourself requires great energy. Maybe you don't think you're up to it, or maybe you give yourself the excuse that you'll do it later. But how much energy do you think you've been expending trying to keep your weaknesses hidden? I promise you'll be amazed at the surge of energy and relaxation you will feel when you begin to release your weaknesses.

Here's an illustration. I once watched a bird that had found a large piece of bread, much larger than what it alone could possibly eat. All the neighboring birds saw the bread and flew down from the trees to partake. The bird expended considerable energy in what we could call selfish maneuvers to keep the bread away from the others. It was so busy taking evasive action that it didn't have time to eat the bread. To me it was obvious that if the bird would have let go of its "selfishness," there would have been enough bread for all and it would have saved an enormous amount of energy just by sharing.

Just so, when you get a larger view of yourself, you will then see the reward of sacrificing your most cherished weaknesses in your increased energy and freedom. Your strengths, alone, are big enough to share with everyone and big enough to confront any situation.

Are the Weaknesses in Others Really in You?

During this process of self-analysis, you may notice that others have weaknesses you don't have. A word of warning: Perhaps another person does indeed have some weaknesses you don't have. But, if you find yourself reacting, especially reacting emotionally to this person's weakness, chances are 99.9% certain that you also have that weakness. For instance, you may find yourself saying, "I just hate the way Julie acts with so little confidence in herself. It seems like she's afraid of her own shadow! I don't even like to be around her, because her fear bothers me so much." There is a good possibility the reason you don't want to be around Julie is because she's acting out *your* fear, *your* lack of confidence. You may be so afraid of this weakness in yourself that you refuse to see it in yourself. Therefore, when you see it in Julie (which you think is safer to do), you react only to Julie when you should be reacting to *yourself* as well.

It's a fact, then, that sometimes our weaknesses are hard to see and remove merely because we are afraid of them. So, let us remove that weakness now. Think of it this way. When you have an ugly wart or growth on your skin, you have no desire to keep it. Even if you hide it from sight, you keep thinking of how you'll get rid of it. Regard your weaknesses the same way. They're not necessarily visible the way warts are, but they are just as "unsightly" and detract from your mental ease and beauty to the same extent.

Anger, fear, resentment, laziness, despair, pessimism, selfishness, revenge, sarcasm, jealousy, worry—these are just a few weak, powerless states of mind to be conquered. When you find yourself reacting with compassion to these characteristics in another or in yourself, you'll know you're well on your way to conquering them. Why? Because compassion is one of the qualities of your Silent Master and signals Its presence beginning to operate in your mind. Compassion also means that you have lost your fear of the weakness, and that is the first step in removing it.

The second step to removing your weakness is to obliterate it by replacing it with a quality that negates it, one that is the opposite of the bad quality. More will be said about this process later. What's important now is to understand that weaknesses are not part of your original self. By replacing your weaknesses with strengths—replacing anger with love, laziness with action, selfishness with selflessness, and so on—you've done everything you need to do to conquer these enemies of your well-being.

2. Learn From Your Mistakes

Mistakes Are Your Feedback System

In the preceding section we discussed how we are constantly evaluating our "on-stage performance" in life and how we tend to hide our weaknesses to put ourselves in a better light, thereby hoping to give ourselves a higher performance rating. For the same reason, we tend to hide our mistakes. Just as we think a good performer can't be weak, we think a good performer cannot make mistakes. So when we do make a mistake, the quicker we get it out of sight and "move on," the better. Think about it for a moment. One of the fastest things we do is cover up a mistake, or excuse it, or justify it. We'll do just about anything to get away from it except look long and hard at it.

Here's the fact about mistakes. They are part of a natural feedback system in learning a task or accomplishing a goal. That's all.

Imagine a gymnastics student learning to do a back flip for the first time. As he strives to imitate the movement as best he can, the teacher tells him two things: what he did correctly, and what he did incorrectly. This is called *positive* and *negative* feedback. The positive feedback describes his right action, and the negative feedback describes his mistakes. Can you see how knowledge of mistakes is just as important in the learning process as knowledge of right actions? When you know what is not correct, you can then consciously strive to avoid the mistake and duplicate the right action. Precise knowledge of *correct* and *incorrect* forms the basis of our conscious choices and actions, and that speeds up the learning process.

Now imagine a person striving to get promoted in her workplace. Perhaps she calls attention to herself by bragging and showing off and calls attention to deficiencies in co-workers to make herself look better. After a while, suddenly she is fired instead of promoted. Did she make a mistake? Absolutely. She must now regard that mistake as feedback on what *not* to do to get a promotion. She still has yet to learn what to do, of course, and may make still more mistakes in the process of finding the right action. But the key is to keep going. She must not let her mistakes be excuses for giving up or for paralyzing future action with self-condemnation. If her goal is worth achieving, she must have the willingness to persist through every form of failure, regarding it always as a learning experience, as feedback, until she hits upon the right action for success.

Making Mistakes Is Making Progress

Willingness to learn from mistakes is the backbone to everything that can be considered progress. How many mistakes do you think Alexander Graham Bell made in inventing the first telephone that connected one room in his house to another? Now telephone technology is developing that will allow you to see the person you're speaking with on the other side of the globe. How many mistakes did the engineers make while developing this technology? Who cares? The object is to succeed, not to count your mistakes.

Mistakes are also essential to your progress. The minute you decide to achieve a goal that's important to you, you will make mistakes. How did we humans get the idea that to be perfect we couldn't make mistakes? Never making a mistake does not make us perfect. Never *repeating* a mistake (after we learn from it) is as perfect as we need to be.

Imagine the freedom you'll feel when you don't have to worry about defending or hiding your mistakes. Experience the increased energy that comes from this freedom! Welcome your mistakes into your consciousness as your friends and teachers.

Fear of Mistakes Is Laziness

Part of our fear of mistakes is pure laziness. What's the worst thing that will happen if you make a mistake? You will have to abandon that course of action and take another, which means, in short, a lot of work. What does that mean? That means you will have to think of another course of action. You may have to be creative. You may have to expend energy in thinking, evaluating, planning. You may have to resist emotions such as despair, futility, rejection, and fear.

If you are mentally lazy, making mistakes will be one of the best excuses you have for giving up, for deciding that maybe your goal isn't so important after all. What a senseless waste that would be. Why expect so little out of life?

Mistakes are not harmful in and of themselves. What is harmful is our attitude toward mistakes. But if you are willing to make mistakes, look at them, regard them as feedback, and keep right on making them until you achieve your goal, then you have the right attitude. You don't purposely make mistakes, of course. But because you are challenging yourself, be aware that mistakes are a natural part of the process.

The right attitude toward mistakes will give you the freedom to pursue your goals with confidence, with minimum distraction, and with your success securely focused in your mind. When you find yourself joyfully moving from one situation to another, using mistakes for learning, growing, and improving, your Silent Master is beginning to operate in your life.

3. We Have the Ability to Do, the Capacity to Act, and the Capability to Perform and Produce

Look again at this Silent Master Image.

II

Your Silent Master Consciousness was born out of the infinite Life Force creating and animating the Universe . . . Because you are this Consciousness, whatever qualities the Life Force possesses, you possess also.

You and the Universe are inseparable; you are a Unit; you are One. The Life Force of the Universe is creative, so you are creative, also. It is the nature of our Universe that thought takes form. Therefore, because you are an integral part of our Universe, your thinking takes form. You have been creating your life since the day you were born.

Remember this image also?

IV

Your Silent Master knows Itself as the Source of mental, emotional, and material Energy—your energy, which you are free to utilize and control in creating what

*you desire. Therefore, you
are a Co-Creator, cooperating with the Life Force of the
Universe to shape yourself
and the world around you.*

The Life Force of the Universe flows through you and beats your heart. When you think, you use Its energy to create other forms of energy, and this energy literally *materializes*—takes form as matter. So, everything material, both objects and events, is a "crystallization" of thought energy. The artist and musician illustrate this process quite naturally. In their work, don't they take an intangible thought or feeling and turn it into something tangible—a painting or a symphony?

You Are an Unlimited Co-Creator

Yes, you already have been creating your life. This process is the gift from the Life Force of the Universe to you.

But your creative process has been largely unconscious and therefore undirected, somewhat haphazard, influenced by other persons' thinking and limited by your restricted awareness of what you think is possible.

The purpose of the third rule of mental conduct is to emphasize how you limit yourself *by yourself*: You limit your thinking with your thinking. This rule tells you to wake up, open up, expand your expectations, and realize you can achieve and produce whatever you can think.

Does that sound too audacious? *Whatever* you can think? Yes. What is it that you *really* want? This is not an invitation to be frivolous in your thinking. If anything, this is a warning to be careful what you think. Why? All thought truly does take form one way or another. There is some truth in the expression, "Be careful what you wish for; you might get it."

Let's exaggerate to make a point: How about blue snow-flakes falling on pink- and yellow-striped rocks in the middle of a desert? Do you realize that such a scene is possible to create with today's electronic video technology? Even that thought has a way to take form. All our modern-day technology has developed progressively to reveal greater capabilities for unlimited expression and communication of thought.

Negative energy creates negative manifestations. Hateful thoughts, for instance, create broken relationships, wars and weapons, physical diseases of all kinds. Positive energy creates positive manifestations. Loving thoughts create harmonious organizations, cooperative governments, and healings of all kinds of discord. It's very simple, really.

What may be difficult is to identify and remove the ways of thinking that produce destructive manifestations. But isn't this why we're here? To learn to take charge of what we manifest by taking charge of our thinking? Can you see now that you can be your own worst enemy? Why? Because you're the one who monitors what you think. Who thinks your thoughts better than you? Others can suggest thoughts to you, but you're the one who accepts or rejects what you entertain in your mind.

Instead, be your own best friend. When you find yourself uncomfortable with your own negative creations and wanting to change your thinking, you are feeling the presence of your Silent Master. Why? Because your discomfort signals that you know something better is possible. Your Silent Master always urges you to grow into greater freedom from limitation of any sort. You may have been willing to accept being poor, being sick, having a job you dislike. Now you know you don't have to accept anything except your freedom, your gift from the Universe to create whatever you desire.

But wherever there is freedom, there must be responsibility. This brings us to the fourth principle of mental conduct.

4. Have Determination and a Quality Purpose

Now we know the law: what we think, we create. The fourth principle tells us how to use our power responsibly in invoking this law.

First, let's talk about the most basic part of this principle: *have* a purpose and determination.

Be Specific

When you decide to make a change, achieve a goal, or create something new in your life, you must focus your objective clearly in your mind. The thought form, "I desire a change in my social life" will take form somehow, but it may be so vague and indistinct that you won't notice a change. "I desire to meet more people" is better; "I desire to meet more people who share my interest in flying airplanes (or whatever)" is better still. Focus as specifically as possible on what you want to accomplish. When you want to buy a car, you identify the make, model, color, and accessories that you desire. When you take a vacation, you plan exactly where you want to go, where you will stay, how you will get there, and proceed to make all the proper arrangements. You are being specific, aren't you? The greater goals in your life deserve as much care, don't they? *Be specific!*

Then, focus your will and unflinching determination behind your purpose.

Determination Depends on You

Here's the unfortunate thing about determination: it works only when you want it to. Let's say you paid a tailor $1,000 in advance to produce evening clothes to wear to a special event. This event will never happen again, and the clothes are only for this evening. Will you go to pick up your new clothes if it's raining? Yes. Will you go if you're angry over a late start because your stew boiled over? Yes. Will you go if you find your street blockaded by road construction? Yes, you'll detour. Will you continue even if the freeway traffic is totally stopped and you have to sit for two hours? Yes. What will you do when you arrive at the tailor's just after he hung the Closed sign? You'll bang on the door until he lets you in.

But, when you're looking for a new job, where does all this determination go after a few rejections? Where does it go when, after more failures than you expected, you give in to fear and dejection? Are your new clothes really so much more deserving of your determination than *you* are?

Unswerving determination is one of the most important factors in reaching your goal, in reaching any goal. Only you can make your determination work for you. And if you use it, your determination will attract to you all the other factors needed for your success—the right associates, the right information, being in the right place at the right time, and so on. Determine now to value determination!

Be a Responsible Creator

The other aspect of this fourth principle is to have a quality purpose. Because we have such great freedom to create, we must take responsibility to use our power constructively.

Remember, you can have whatever you can think. This even holds true for the person plotting to rob a bank. This plan may certainly take material form and "succeed," but other thoughts that are the foundation for the decision to rob the bank will also take form, thoughts such as I am a have-not; I am a victim; I have nothing to contribute to society; I am wanted by the law, hunted and pursued; I am so worthless, poor and powerless, I have to steal to get money . . . All these thoughts and more will ultimately take form as a literal prison or, if not apprehended, as a prison of poverty, despair, fear, and loneliness. Yet, this person has free will and creates exactly what is thought.

Clearly, however, this person does not have a "quality" purpose.

Your true desires, those longings for certain goals that feel like a part of you, are given to you from your Silent Master. Therefore, you have every right to put your purpose, will, and determination behind them to make them manifest. But if you ever have any doubt about whether a certain desire is worthy of your total energy and attention, look at the supporting beliefs behind that desire. That will give you your answer.

For instance, you may say, "I desire to build a new house." Let's consider two different sets of supporting thoughts behind this desire. First, suppose you say, "I want a new house because my brother has a better one than I have." If this is so, be prepared to manifest some other unsavory thoughts that are necessarily part of this picture such as, I'm not valuable in and of myself; my worth is measured by how well I stand up to someone else. I am never quite as good as someone else so I constantly have to play catch-up. My decisions are based on what I have to do to compete, not on what I really want to do; therefore, I don't make my own decisions; I'm too busy reacting instead of acting. I don't value who I am so I feel the need to be jealous. Do you see how far-reaching a single thought or desire can be?

On the other hand, suppose you say, "I want a new

house because my family members and I need more space and privacy to pursue our individual projects without interfering with each other." Supporting thoughts that are part of this picture include, My family and I are pursuing worthwhile activities. We respect individual differences, and we believe we should follow the path of our choosing unobstructed. We value family harmony. There is room for individuals to fulfill their needs while also being part of a group. A growing and expanding house supports our ability to grow and expand as people. Would you like to manifest all these thoughts as well as the new house? I think so.

Do you see now the importance of identifying the supporting thoughts behind your desire? You will manifest those thoughts as well as your desire! Generally, you know your desire is true and coming from your Silent Master when you have a calm sense of peace when you visualize your desire in your mind. You will have a feeling not unlike love when you think about this desire.

If your desire then passes the test of looking at all its supporting thoughts, then throw all your energy into making it happen. You now know that you *can* make it manifest! You can. This ability is a gift from the Universe to you, a fundamental law of your being.

5. Have a Positive Mental Attitude

Emotions Have Creative Power

Thus far, we've emphasized mental activities occurring in the "thinking" part of your consciousness. There is also a "feeling" part of you, the part of your consciousness that experiences emotion. Your feelings and emotions play a large role in what you manifest or fail to manifest. If you think of your thoughts as seeds, think of your emotional environment as soil. Therefore, your positive seeds must be sown in positive soil to grow and flourish. Together, your positive thoughts and feelings create a *positive mental attitude*. The fifth principle of mental conduct emphasizes how this state of mind is essential for your success.

Note how we can use the word "attitude" almost interchangeably with the phrase "state of mind." An attitude is a mental focus and consists of thoughts, beliefs, and emotions (feelings), all of which will result in some kind of behavior. Your behavior, then, reflects all the qualities of your attitude. Why? Because that which is called your attitude is a creative force behind your actions and creations.

The word "attitude" comes from the Latin root word *aptitudo*, which means "fitness" or "aptitude." So "attitude" is literally related to the concept of aptitude or capability. How true. Your attitude has everything to do with what you are capable of achieving. Therefore, in this section, we will carefully analyze how to create this positive attitude that is responsible for your success and achievement.

Here again is an Image of your Silent Master consciousness:

IV

---

*Your Silent Master knows
Itself as the Source of
mental,* emotional, *and
material* Energy—*your
Energy, which you are free to
utilize and control in
creating what you desire.*

Emotions are batteries of power; they contribute tremendous energy in the creative process of transforming thought into form. Your emotions are your friends when they constructively accompany and support your creative thinking. They are your enemies when they sabotage and conflict with your mental objectives. If you are trying to make a change in your life or achieve a goal, you may need to clear away some negative feelings, even if those feelings are unrelated to your goal. You may be trying to create a new career and thinking quite positively about it; but if your emotional condition is presently full of anger and resentment over a broken relationship, for instance, this negative emotional soil will not help your new thought-seeds grow.

Here is an important point to help you understand your emotions. Emotions don't come out of nowhere; they follow thoughts. The positive or negative emotions you feel are a result of an idea you have first. If you are feeling the emotion of anger, the thought creating the emotion may be something like, I am thwarted; I am being deceived; I don't get my way. The feeling of affection may be created by, I value this person's honesty; I desire to express my appreciation.

Sometimes, however, your emotions do appear to come out of nowhere, and sometimes they seem to conflict with what you're thinking. You may say, "I'm thinking as positively as I can about this situation, but I'm still depressed." What's wrong? If thought *creates* emotion, how is it possible to have emotions that conflict with your thinking? The answer is, you may have formed *invisible* thoughts that are now creating emotions.

You Have a Conscious and a Subconscious Mind

To understand where invisible thoughts come from, you must realize that you have a conscious mind (accessible to your immediate awareness) and a subconscious mind (outside of your immediate awareness). The prefix "sub" means underneath; so by definition, you have thoughts and feelings "underneath" your conscious mind, which you are not aware of. You are, however, affected by these thoughts and feelings. Although you are not aware of them, they still operate.

What is your subconscious mind? It is a storehouse of everything you have experienced—all your thoughts, feelings, memories; all the programming you've experienced since you were born. It is like an amazingly accurate video and audio tape recorder of your entire experience. It is *sub*-conscious because your conscious mind was not designed to hold this volume of information. Your conscious mind has a different responsibility: it processes only the information you need to function in the present moment. To open a soda can, you don't need to remember the color of the baby crib you slept in (which is stashed away in your subconscious).

Fortunately, your conscious mind can "ask" your subconscious mind for information, and the information can suddenly become conscious. Your conscious mind is similar to the cursor on a computer screen. It goes where you direct it. "What was the name of that blond-haired girl I liked in the second grade?" you may wonder. While you're doing the dishes two days later, you suddenly remember. Or, "Why is it that when I see Tom, I feel like painting?" You may suddenly become aware that Tom looks exactly like an old friend in your high school art class. Note that the cursor (your conscious mind) doesn't need to know the contents of the program or how the computer functions (your total consciousness); its only function is to select and focus.

Sometimes, however, subconscious information is difficult to obtain precisely because you don't know everything that's in it. Remember: by definition, it's outside your conscious awareness. You may not know what information to ask for. When this happens, conflicts between your thoughts and emotions occur.

Here's an illustration. Let's suppose you are in a martial arts training program, and have to give up drinking alcoholic beverages. Clearly, you have a quality purpose and determination, and everything is going well in your training. At your workplace nothing has changed. Yet, you notice that whenever you have a conference with your boss, you have an irresistible desire to go home and drink until you're relaxed or "high." Despite your best efforts and will power, you give in to this urge each time, and you don't know why. Now you feel miserable and depressed, which *does* affect your training.

The probable cause is subconscious programming. You could have a memory of infant anxiety being quelled by drinking. Subconsciously—*not* consciously—you remember that every time you were anxious, uncomfortable, upset, and crying, you received a bottle of comforting liquid that stopped the crying and solved all your problems. Let's be clear, now. We're not talking about satisfying your physical thirst. We're talking about escape from anxiety.

In this example, the conferences with your boss are stimulating feelings of discomfort and anxiety that you are not facing in an effective manner. Hence, the old programming kicks in, and you find yourself seeking out the same solution: drinking a liquid that kills pain, just as milk comforted you long ago.

In this example, you are totally unaware of this programming. Here you are, putting forth all your energy to give up alcohol, and you're being sabotaged by invisible thoughts about how to relieve pain. Because you're not aware of what's going on, you don't attack the real cause of the problem; you attack yourself instead. "I'm weak," you may say. "I have no will power. I am a failure." The result is feelings of dejection, futility, and condemnation—*not* a positive mental attitude. Your goal cannot be reached under these circumstances. You have a conflict. Your mind is saying "I desire to give up alcohol." Your emotions are saying, "I feel helpless and powerless because I can't do it."

Help for Your Subconscious Programming

When this happens, you can turn to your Silent Master Consciousness. It operates over both your conscious and subconscious mind. Remember this image of your Silent Master:

v

---

*Your Silent Master is
completely aware, infinitely
Intelligent, and ready to
give you all the insight,
information, and direction you
need to fulfill your dreams,
ambitions, and goals . . .*

You can affirm that you and your Silent Master are One. Then, by simply *knowing* you have this unlimited awareness and intelligence available to you, you can ask for information regarding your obstacle, whatever it may be. Asking is as simple as mentally posing the question to yourself and expecting the answer to come into your conscious awareness. However long or short a time it takes, the answer will surely come. You may be led to persons, books, or situations that will ultimately assist you, and you *will* get your answer.

Remember, your real self already knows Its freedom from mental and emotional limitations. Thus, you can insist on experiencing the feelings of your real self. These are always positive feelings that you can claim as your own!

Yes, there are reasons why such positive emotions as joy, optimism, love, compassion, affection, hope, and gratitude help you achieve your goals. They bring forth the presence of your Silent Master Consciousness, and therefore they have creative power. A positive mental attitude means that you are free from conflicting thoughts and emotions. You feel emotions of joy, peace, and confidence, because you *expect* success. You feel strong, because you realize you have power, and you have removed (or are removing) all negative thoughts and emotions that could obstruct your manifestation.

Your emotions constantly give you feedback about the quality of your thinking. You can consciously strive to entertain thoughts that bring you the most positive feelings.

How to Deal with Negative Emotions

You may be thinking, That's all theoretically encouraging, but right now I feel depressed (or some other negative emotional state). What do I do right now?

When you feel negative, first acknowledge that you feel negative. That may seem overly simplistic, but you'd be surprised how often you refuse to acknowledge that you're feeling angry or depressed. There will always be some deeper, covert manifestations of ignored emotions—such as developing a headache instead of expressing your anger—and as an effective emotion-dodger, you'll say that the physical symptom is due to some other cause. Be very aware that you may have become quite expert at denying emotions, which creates quite a Pandora's Box of physical illnesses, misdirected reactions, covert aggression, and inexplicable emotional outbursts. (Also, ask yourself if you deny your good feelings as well. Many times trying to push away bad feelings causes us to push away *all* emotion, including our positive feelings.)

After you acknowledge the presence of the negative feeling, next remember that you have three options. Choose the third option and avoid the first two.

Option 1: Carving in Wood or Stone

Perhaps you may have immortalized a romance between you and a girlfriend or boyfriend by carving your names in a tree trunk or in wet cement. The idea was to make the symbol permanent. You may have already carved some negative emotional states, such as anger, worry, resentment, fear, or sorrow, into your consciousness. These emotions are coming from either your conscious or your subconscious mind. You may have felt so righteously justified in feeling them that you accepted them and had no intention of letting them go. But whom does this really affect? It hurts only you. Perhaps when you adopted these negative feelings, you didn't know that this option would eventually obstruct your growth.

Option 2: Writing in Sand

The native Americans created sand drawings, knowing full well that ultimately the wind would blow them away. This is how I describe negative emotions that are held until something external happens to stimulate them or change them. We haven't determined to keep them, but likewise we haven't determined to release them. This is an unstable emotional condition because we are not "in charge" of those emotions and we don't take constructive action to neutralize the negative feelings. Maybe the emotions will be discharged smoothly; maybe they won't. But their presence, until removed, is counterproductive and obstructive.

Option 3: Writing in Water

We cannot write in water. We cannot carve in water. Water's nature is to flow. And that is how we should treat negative emotion. When it comes, let it go. Let it flow away from you like water moving down a river bed. Do not allow it to reside in your consciousness for any amount of time or to become permanent. Release it as soon as it comes. "I can't," you may say. Your Silent Master says you can. No matter how intense an emotion may be, if you *immediately* refuse to dwell on it and refuse to focus on it, it will have no staying power. Speed is the key. Act quickly to release it.

How is this different from covering up an emotion? You acknowledge that you are feeling it, but immediately let it flow through and away from you. You do not deny it, but you do release it.

Bear in mind that to some extent you may enjoy your negative emotional states. Be willing to admit that perhaps you've found them comfortable, familiar friends. Yes, on the surface you may say that it's no fun being angry. But are you sure? Are you sure there are no payoffs such as, When I'm angry I like the feeling of being "right"; When I'm depressed, my husband pays more attention to me. (Manipulating others through negative states is what I call emotional blackmail.)

Positive Emotions Come From Your Real Self

On the other hand, if you truly find yourself growing more and more uncomfortable with your negative emotions, if they are annoying distractions to this little flame of peace and well-being starting to glow within you, if you find yourself wanting to nurture even the smallest, most quiet feeling of self-appreciation, if you find yourself wanting, really wanting, to be happy within yourself, you are feeling your Silent Master. You have already met each other. You can know now that this little manifestation of real feeling is destined to unfold into the whole consciousness of love, peace, harmony, and creative power.

All you need to do is harness this unfolding power, hold onto it, and let it grow. Then consciously work to replace your negative emotional patterns with feelings that support your goal, whatever it may be. You have heard that nothing succeeds like success? It is so. Every real feeling expands and creates more positive feelings. Capture this momentum. Because your Silent Master is the Consciousness of Love, and because you are your Silent Master, love yourself! Lift yourself out of your negative emotional patterns with determination and total commitment.

Remember:

VI

Your Silent Master expresses
completeness, fulfillment,
harmony, peace, joy, and
love, and imparts these
qualities to everything
It creates.

Three Tools of the Jung SuWon Warrior

You become a warrior in Jung SuWon as soon as you begin practicing the preceding five principles of mental conduct. They will prepare you to use the seven basic principles of inner power—the keys to creative thinking—which appear in the next chapter.

For now, just as a traditional warrior carries tools or weapons appropriate to his profession, here are three tools that will accompany you throughout your entire practice of Jung SuWon.

BALANCE—AWARENESS—VISUALIZATION

The knowledge of balance will be the armor you wear so you can travel fearlessly through any experience life brings to you. Awareness will be the shield you use to deflect that which you do not need or want. Visualization will be the sword you use to cut through worn, outmoded, or negative forms to make room for the new.

1. BALANCE

Unity Through Polarity: Yin and Yang

What holds the atoms of this book together? What keeps them from flying apart and disintegrating this book? In the simplest terms of classical physics, the atoms in this book are held together by a polarized force composed of equal and opposite electrical charges called protons and electrons. In the nucleus of each atom is a positive charge that is counterbalanced by an equal negative charge created by the orbiting electrons. Each atom is thereby unified and stabilized.

This is one of nature's manifestations of a great fundamental principle of the Universe: namely, Unity through Polarity. This principle is depicted in oriental philosophies, including Jung SuWon, as the yin-yang symbol:

This symbol was designed to describe the nature of the Life Force of the Universe and everything created by it. It is a symbol of the oneness and interrelatedness of all creation.

The circle taken as a whole also tells us that the Life Force of the Universe operates via two equal and opposite forces, which manifest in some form on every level of our life experience. That is, we experience the manifestations of yin and yang forces mentally, materially, spiritually, and physically. We see these forces in operation in the entire material world.

The white half of the circle represents the yang force; the black half represents the yin force. Note that although they are equal and opposite, they are inextricably bound together as *one*. They do not—and cannot—exist independently of each other. Also note that a portion of the yin force appears in the yang force, symbolized by a tiny black circle within the white half, and vice versa. We will later see this has great significance.

First let's look at a few qualities and concepts manifested by these two forces to see how they differ. Then we'll see how they blend and harmonize in a complementary fashion.

Yang	*Yin*
Male	Female
Creative (giving)	Receptive (receiving)
Aggressive	Passive
Strong	Weak
Heaven	Earth
White	Black
Hot	Cool
Light (radiating)	Dark (absorbing)
Thrusting	Yielding
Day	Night
Open	Hidden
Increase	Decrease
Fullness	Emptiness

To some extent we could say that these qualities or concepts are opposite. Rather than thinking of them as opposites, however, think of them as giving rise to each other. This happens in two ways. First, we can say that fullness gives rise to the concept of emptiness, because fullness automatically, by one definition, means that which is *not empty*; so in a way, fullness automatically creates the concept of emptiness. As you go down the list, you can see that this holds true for the other words.

But there is another way these qualities give rise to each other. Do you notice in the yin-yang symbol that the black half increases in size until it "flows into" the small portion of the white half? The white then increases and flows into the small portion of the dark half. This means that when the yang force increases, there is a point at which it can increase no further, and then it "becomes" yin.

Here's an example that shows yin and yang at work in your body. You've noticed that you are energetic and active for a period (yang increasing), but at a certain point you must allow your energy *to turn into* relaxation and quiet. Being relaxed and quiet is the yin state, and when that state is fulfilled, it flows into the yang state and you become active again. The yin and yang states *balance* your energy so that you are neither dangerously over-exerting nor stagnantly passive.

You can think of activity and rest as opposites, but it's more accurate to say that they give rise to each other, turn into each other, complement each other, and create harmony and balance.

Thus, the dot of white in the black yin area symbolizes that the yin force carries the "seed" of the yang force within it, so that at the right time yin is destined to turn into yang. The yang force likewise has the seed of the yin force within it and will ultimately become yin.

Think again now about this Silent Master Image:

II

Your Silent Master Consciousness was born out of

48

the infinite Life Force creat-
ing and animating the Uni-
verse. You exist as part of
the Universe; therefore, It is
the Life Force creating and
animating you. Because you
are this Consciousness,
whatever qualities the Life
Force possesses, you possess
also.

Consciousness Expresses Qualities of Yin and Yang

Because the yin-yang symbol describes the Life Force of the Universe, it also describes your Silent Master Conscious-ness, which contains all the qualities, all the potential of both yin and yang. You have the capability to express either one at the appropriate time to maintain balance in any situ-ation. A man, as a biological expression of the yang force, will tend to manifest the strong, "aggressive" qualities asso-ciated with it; but in a balanced state of mind, he is also capable of expressing the receptive, yielding qualities of the female yin force when appropriate.

Your Real Self is a perfect balance of yin and yang quali-ties, and true freedom is the freedom to express the qualities of both. Yet, many are discouraged from expressing the qualities associated with the opposite sex. In most cultures, many yang qualities have been assigned to male social roles and many yin qualities to female social roles. In a confron-tation on the job, for instance, a man has the right to ex-press the quiet, receptive sensitivity of the female yin state without being labeled "weak"; a woman has the right to ex-press the penetrating, aggressive power of the male yang force without being labeled a "battle-axe." Appropriate action is always the key.

Your Silent Master Consciousness knows whether a yin or yang action is needed to create balance in any situation. Thus, you must cultivate the qualities of both so that you can act appropriately. In the next section I talk more about how to listen to your Silent Master Consciousness so that you are guided into correct action.

Perhaps the most obvious manifestation of yin and yang in action is *change*. The motion of these two forces in the world are seen in rhythms of change such as day and night, the ebb and flow of the tides, the changing of seasons, birth and death, death and regeneration, seed and harvest.

There are also rhythms of change in our bodies. Much has been written about biological rhythms, periods of increased and decreased energy that can affect our health and disposition. Some studies have helped employers create work shifts that harmonize with these rhythms. And there are rhythms of change in our lives. If you look closely, you can see when there have been times of progress followed by stagnation followed by increase, prosperity followed by lack followed by abundance, joy followed by sorrow followed by happiness, and so on.

Maintain Balance Through the Flow of Yin and Yang

Why is the knowledge of balance and change a tool? Because when you know there are cycles of change, you avoid accepting limited or negative conditions as permanent or final. No matter where you are in a cycle, the seed for the new condition is there.

But just because that seed is present does not mean it will always automatically develop. In the cycle of seed and harvest, for example, the harvest does not arrive automatically. The farmer must work the land, plant the seeds, and provide the water. When you desire a change, you must do the work of *choosing* to bring about the change and support your choice with appropriate actions.

It's easy to want to change a bad condition into a good one, and easy to make the choice to do so. But what about when a good condition changes into a bad one and you didn't choose that? The knowledge of balance and change is a tool here as well. This knowledge helps you keep your perspective when changes you didn't expect occur. For instance, now you know that times of increase and fullness carry the seeds of decrease and emptiness—that in times of abundance you may find that some form of decrease occurs. But, you also know that with this decrease, there is inevitably the seed of a new increase, meant to give you even more than you had before. Decrease and emptiness are not necessarily negative states. They may be serving a purpose: to take away that which may be standing in your way of greater good.

Thus, there is another law associated with these laws of change: Unending Progress. This law affirms that the whole purpose of change, the whole purpose of continuous cycles of yin and yang is to take you higher, to make you grow, to give you more of what will lead you to a truer expression of your Real Self.

Your Silent Master Consciousness, then, urges you to have an attitude of letting go. You needn't hold on to positive or negative conditions as though they will last forever; rather, let the flow from yin to yang to yin lead you into harmonious, balanced, progressive change. Never be afraid of change. By letting go and listening to your Silent Master, all change should lead you into greater good. That is the purpose of change and the purpose of life.

2. AWARENESS

The Voice of the Silent Master

I said before that your Silent Master Consciousness knows when a yin or yang action is called for to create balance. Yet, how often we find ourselves making the wrong move, increasing discord rather than eliminating it. You may even have had moments where you said, "If only I had listened to myself, I wouldn't have done that."

You were probably right. You may not have been aware of it, but your Silent Master Consciousness appears to speak to you very quietly sometimes, through a faculty we call *intuition*.

When you have an intuition, it feels like an impulse to say or do something that suddenly pops into your conscious mind. Generally, an intuition will feel like a right choice and will bring you a sense of serenity or peaceful resolution (even if you may not have wanted to do it). It may feel very vague, as if it's not really your own thought. But it is. This inner "voice" is actually your inner knowing. It is your Silent Master's knowing attempting to penetrate your consciousness with Its truth. It does not necessarily speak softly; It only appears to do so because your surface thoughts and emotions noisily clamor for so much attention. Clearly, if you could consistently be aware of these leadings from your Silent Master, you could make the right moves at the right time. How, then, can you develop greater awareness of this supremely intelligent, quiet voice?

Ideally, your awareness should be like a pool of still water. Light travels easily into still water, and you can see right into it. It becomes very clear. But when the wind blows and the water is agitated, or when the water is polluted, you can't see what's in it clearly. So, how can you make your mind like a pool of still, clean water, undisturbed by turbulent surface thoughts, free from polluting feelings and emotions, so that the light of your Silent Master Consciousness travels easily into your awareness?

Listening to Your Silent Master

The first step is to develop the ability to let go, as we discussed previously, to refuse to hold onto any condition as being permanent. In the same way that a river keeps itself clean by staying in motion, let negative thoughts and emotions flow away as quickly as they come. This takes courage, but don't be afraid. When you can let your thoughts and emotions come and go freely, you keep your mind swept clean of obstructing mental debris. How can you hear your Silent Master this very moment if your mind is occupied with yesterday's resentment? Or today's panic? Or tomorrow's anticipation? Or with fear, worry, and anger?

This brings us to the second step: Living in the NOW. Your Silent Master speaks to you always in the present moment, because *now* is all there is. Therefore, *now* is where reality is, and *now* is where the creative moment is.

Why is now the only creative moment? When it was yesterday, you experienced it as *now*. When you experience tomorrow, it will be *now*. At this moment, and every moment thereafter, it is *now*. It is never tomorrow or yesterday. What are you thinking right now? What concepts and emotions are you holding right now? Whatever they are, they are in the present moment and on their way to becoming manifest.

The key to listening to your Silent Master and creating harmony in all your life is to *live only in the present moment*. Do you do that? Don't be surprised if you find that an examination of your thought habits reveals that you never or hardly ever live in the present moment. When it is now, how often are you mentally somewhere else, thinking or worrying about what just happened or what's going to happen? Is your mental video recorder constantly playing pictures of the past and concerns for the future? If so, you are giving up your creative power in the present moment.

Awareness Happens Only Now

True awareness means being right where you are, right now, without fear or worry or obsession about the future or past. When you manage to do that, a wonderful thing happens. Focused here, now, you become undistracted. You find yourself becoming mentally quiet. And when that happens, you "hear" your Silent Master quite clearly. You perceive all around you quite clearly. You find yourself knowing what to do—now, ten minutes from now, or tomorrow. As a result, you consistently find yourself in the right place at the right time. Why? Because living in the present moment is an act of surrender to the greater intelligence of your Silent Master, the greater intelligence of life itself. In this listening state, moment by moment you feel and respond to Its promptings. It is "guiding" you; we can also say that you and your Silent Master are moving together as One.

"I have to plan," you may say. "I have to think about what I'm going to do ten minutes from now, or tomorrow, or it won't happen." Yes, you should make plans in the present moment. You don't ever stop thinking, but be watchful to keep yourself open to new incoming ideas that may change what you plan. The point is to be *aware* every moment of what you are thinking, because whatever is going on now is on the way to manifesting. How important it is, then, to keep everything you don't want out of your moment-to-moment consciousness. How can you do that if you're not focused here, now?

When you can seize control of the now moment, you take intelligent control of your life.

3. Visualization

When I was a young girl in Korea, I was fascinated by a flower that bloomed only at night. Appropriately, they were called moon flowers. As I sat in the garden at night watching them open, I was amazed that even in the moonlight their color was so beautiful. I remember having the thought that surely our ideas of color came from Nature. I thought, How often people look at flowers or a beautiful sunset and want to imitate these colors somehow, in art, in clothing, or whatever. Isn't it interesting that the purity of nature, its original natural beauty, inspires us to capture it or duplicate it? Certainly, this is one form of visualization: reproducing in representative ways what we see in the world around us.

Ideas are quite invisible when compared to moon flowers or sunsets. Yet, they are just as real and just as inspiring! Do we not feel excited about a new idea just as we do when we experience the rare and beautiful in Nature? When we experience true ideas, we are likewise naturally impelled to capture their beauty in material form.

Ideas Create Images

Remember this Image of your Silent Master Consciousness:

I
_____

*Your Silent Master is your
Real Self, your original Self.*

It expresses Itself through
your thinking, through true
Ideas and Thoughts in your
mind . . .

These ideas are the primal, original source of everything that manifests in visible form. In fact, the word "idea" is derived from the Greek root word that means "to see," so an idea automatically carries with it the concept of visibility. Haven't you noticed that when you understand an idea, you usually say, "I see." In our universe, we turn ideas into material form. Visualization is a powerful tool for doing so.

Visualization is the process of forming a *mental image*, and the process of forming images in our mind is called imagining (something most of us do with relative ease).

The word "image" comes from the same Latin root as the word "imitate." This means that when we form an image, we are imitating or creating a likeness of something else. That something else is an idea. All images, whether those you see outside you or those you see in your mind's eye, are visible duplications of some idea.

Ideas and Images Take Form

Let's take a simple idea, like "comfort." We can be very creative in turning that idea into form. What images come to your mind? A kind of chair? Some kind of house or car? A person? A geographical location or climate? Certain kinds of clothes? A bank account of a certain size? Clearly, comfort can take many visible forms. (Remember now, we are talking about true comfort, not the distorted sense of comfort such as taking drugs to escape from reality.)

Suppose someone were to look around and say, "I do not have the comfort of certain objects in my life." Again we're back to that original question, Who am I? This person has answered, "*I am not comfortable.*"

What a strange and contradictory belief, however! In the process of stating this negative condition, she has affirmed the potential existence of the positive. She has said, "I am not *comfortable*," which means she knows the idea of comfort. And, if she knows it, she can have it. This is true of any idea. If you can think it, you can have it. You may have to work hard in making some mental and emotional changes to manifest it. But you can have it.

I use this example to show that most of your negative statements are exactly like this. I am not financially stable; I am not happy; I am not healthy means that you know the ideas of financial stability, happiness, and health. So if they have not taken visible, tangible form, you may not have used your power of visualization to support their manifestation.

Let's go back to this person who says "I am not comfortable." She sees herself working at a job she dislikes for which she's underpaid; she sees herself coming home to an apartment that is much too small, with inadequate furnishings because she can't afford better; she sees herself going into debt to make ends meet. If you ask her to start a program of literally imagining herself in a job she wants, living in a spacious apartment or home, and having all the money required, she may become angry and tell you that that's impractical daydreaming. "Look at the visible facts. I have to be realistic."

To be "realistic," however, is to know that all visible manifestations follow the ideas and images you hold in your mind.

Consider again:

III
_____

Your Silent Master Consciousness knows Itself to be

57

*immaterial in substance,
but It also takes form
(manifests) as your physical body and the material
world around you. Thus,
you may describe yourself as
being both immaterial (spiritual) and material (physical)
at the same time.*

Effective Visualization

The practice of creative visualization is not idle day-dreaming or wishful thinking. Yes, you could say that it's like dreaming, but it's more than that. It is *focused* imagining, with the power of your will and persistence behind it. It is an immaterial activity that takes form first as a mental image, then as a material image.

Visualization is the first step in bringing forth your quality purpose and determination (the fourth principle of mental conduct); therefore, you must exercise responsibility in what you imagine. You use the same responsibility you used when you formed your quality purpose and determination.

The mental images you form must absolutely support what you want to create and should be visualized with as much detail and clarity as possible. If you give equal time to images contrary to your objective, it would be like trying to dig a hole and fill it at the same time.

Unfortunately, when we have idle time, many of us have a habit of running all sorts of negative pictures through our minds. But now that you are aware that visualization is a powerful part of the creative process, use this wonderful tool to lend momentum to achieving your goals! Allow only those images in your mind that support you and others, and see how quickly things change.

If your ideas are different from what everyone else thinks, it does not necessarily mean that you're wrong. Most flowers bloom in the sun and close at night. The moon flower is an exception. We certainly cannot consider it "wrong" for blooming in the moonlight.

Armed with these three tools—the knowledge of balance, awareness, and visualization—let us move on to the seven principles of inner power.

CHAPTER 4

Becoming One With Your Silent Master

SEVEN STEPS TO INNER POWER

Your Silent Master Consciousness is already a part of you. To claim Its power and intelligence, to become One with your Silent Master, you must identify with It. If you wish, you may think of your Silent Master as another "frequency" of your consciousness that your mind can attune to.

Here again is a Silent Master Image for you to consider:

IV

Your Silent Master knows Itself as the Source of . . . your Energy, which you are free to utilize and control in creating what you desire. Therefore, you are a Co-Creator, cooperating with

61

the Life Force of the Uni-
verse to shape yourself and
the world around you.

So, when you attune to your Silent Master Consciousness, you connect with the Source of great creative power. But how do you do that? How do you identify with the Silent Master within yourself so that It becomes your "I"?

By thinking as It thinks.

In this chapter, I will give you seven principles, seven ways of thinking that help your consciousness attune to and open to your Silent Master Consciousness. You do not have to strive for power. Your creative power will unfold and develop automatically as you begin using these seven principles, because they will cause you to think as your Silent Master does.

I give these principles to you in this particular order because each one helps you develop the next.

1. Body and Mind as One

As we stated before:

III

Your Silent Master Con-
sciousness knows Itself to be
immaterial in substance, but
It also takes form (mani-
fests) as your physical body
and the material world
around you. Thus, you may
describe yourself as being
both immaterial (spiritual)

and material (physical) at
the same time.

The key words now are "at the same time." Simply to know that your body and your personal world around you are created by thought, emotion, and visualization does much to help you take creative control of your life. Certainly this is the starting point.

Next, however, just as you discipline your mind (your mental and spiritual thinking), you must discipline your body (your physical action) to conform to your mental objectives. Your bodily actions must be at one with your mental efforts.

Remember how we discussed that holding negative visual images opposed to your positive visual images is like digging a hole and filling it at the same time? It's a counterproductive process to say the least. In the same way, if your physical actions don't support your mental objectives, you sabotage your efforts. Conversely, you increase your momentum when all your physical actions support your goals.

As the Silent Master Image tells us, your body *is* your mind; that is, your body is a material picture of concepts in your mind. Therefore, your body will have a natural propensity to conform to your thinking. You will have a natural inclination to take physical actions that are in accord with your thinking.

In reality, you don't think *about* your body. Your thinking *is* your body. But, if you insist on regarding your body as separate from your mind, this belief will take form as your body being outside your control. Your belief of separateness will cause your body to seemingly have a separate "mind" of its own, and then it can say things like "I am ill; I am too weak to do this or that; I can't; I won't. . ." and so on. This mistaken belief of a separate mind and body does not change reality, but it certainly denies it and you lose your power.

To claim your unity with your Silent Master Consciousness, you must *know* that your mind and body are one. Your mind and body are different aspects, different manifestations, different "frequencies" of the same Life Force. Knowing this, you can take charge of your body and cause it to do and be what you need.

Because your body and mind are one, they are in intimate communication with each other. You can look at your body and gain insight into the quality of your thinking; and you can look at your thinking to determine how to shape and direct your body. Doesn't a healthy tree produce healthy fruit? Just so, when your thoughts are healthy, your body reflects this condition. Conversely, when you're ill, it may be helpful to examine your state of mind or the state of your beliefs to locate the cause of your illness.

Your body is the living temple of your consciousness. As a manifestation of your Silent Master Consciousness, your body is a holy place and deserving of your utmost love, care, and respect. Your body is meant to be well and whole and to beautifully carry out the instructions of your mind like a faithful servant.

Your body and mind, then, are designed to act as one at all times. This may take much focus, determination, and concentration on your part. For instance, you may set a goal of winning a marathon race. Your mind says, "This is an important priority; I want to win; I want to use all my spare time building up my speed and endurance by practicing every day." If you nevertheless insist on partying often to late hours, eating improperly, skipping workouts "just this one time," accepting frivolous invitations instead of turning them down, and on and on, is your body at one with your mind? How likely are you to succeed under these circumstances? Clearly, if this race is a priority, if you truly want to win, you will have to take control of your body and make all your physical activity conform to your goal. Body and mind as one!

Remember, what you do with every moment of *now* is all that matters. There will never be a tomorrow to realize your goals. When you know your mind and body are one right now and only right now, when you let this principle reach into every aspect of your living experience, then you will be in the driver's seat, and you take control. You are thinking as your Silent Master thinks.

Body and Mind as One leads next to Truth.

2. Truth

Truth is Self-discovery. As you develop the habit of regarding your body and life experience as pictures of your thinking, you will certainly begin to learn something about yourself. Isn't this what we call the moment of truth?

What are your strengths? What are your weaknesses? What do you see?

Before going further, let's review another Silent Master Image:

I

Your Silent Master is your Real Self, your original Self. . . . It is your eternal Selfhood that exists apart from your brain (which is a sensory processor only) and the personality traits imposed on you from your environment.

Have you created your self mostly with information coming from outside yourself? The answer may not be clear. Be very honest. In the first chapter, I mentioned dependency as being one of the first concepts you developed, and I discussed how your early dependency on others may have caused you to conform to their expectations about you.

Furthermore, the culture you are raised in also affects your self-concept. The same person could develop a different view of himself if he were raised in tribal Africa or in the Soviet Union, because he would be exposed to different religious, political, and social ideas; all these ideas shape how we see our place in the world. So, isn't it possible you may have listened more to outside sources than to yourself in forming your self-image and, as a result, lost sight of some of your real qualities?

There is another factor that causes you to lose touch with yourself: relying solely on the evidence of your five material senses to tell you who you are. Your senses of taste, touch, smell, hearing, and sight are wonderful processors of sensory information, but they are not the source of your intelligence. They are channels for your intelligence to flow through so that you can materially experience what you create—and that's all.

Let's take a person who believes she is physically weak. Perhaps as the youngest child in a family, she was unable to defend herself against the advances of older siblings and consequently developed the concept that she couldn't be strong. Sure enough, her belief took form as a weak, underdeveloped body. Now, as she looks out through her eyes and feels through her undeveloped muscles, all the sensory information going through her brain says, "I am weak."

But is she? That's what her brain says, but it's not what her Silent Master says. The truth is, strength is one of the ideas in the Silent Master Consciousness; therefore she can express that idea.

The key word is "express," which literally means to "press outward." This person has a right to claim the idea of strength as belonging to her and press this idea outward into material form, into a body that *expresses* strength.

The opposite of this process is being "*impressed*," which literally means to "press inward." This is what evidence gained through the five senses does. Daily our senses are bombarded with all kinds of sensations: screeching sounds that jar us, unkind words that affect us, smiles that make us happy. Whether good or bad, these images and sensations from outside *impress* us with a feeling of hard reality, making us feel that we can't change things. This can certainly *de*-press us. But because all outside images were first created as thoughts, new thoughts can create new images. We can change things, no matter what the sensory information in our brains tells us. However, we are not likely to create new thoughts if we are easily impressed with images and concepts coming to us from outside ourselves and if we regard that information as the final word.

The Silent Master Consciousness wants only to *express* Its beautiful ideas into form. Therefore, no material picture is the final statement, because the material picture is not the original reality. Ideas are the only real, enduring reality. As we express ideas, they may take many forms. Ideas are the cause. Material forms are the effect.

Thus, when you look at your weaknesses, your limitations, your obstacles, you're looking at the "effects" of incorrect ideas about yourself. When you *know* these effects are not the real you, you will think as your Silent Master thinks.

The Truth is that the only ideas about you that are real are ideas that express beauty, power, dominion, strength, love, wisdom, clarity, and perfection—ideas in your Silent Master Consciousness. You express your Silent Master when you look past the sensory information processed through your brain and look only to those unlimited ideas as the source and manifestation of your True Self. As you identify yourself with these ideas, see how easily you move from one stage of development to another, setting higher and higher goals because, in truth, you are not limited.

Truth leads to Purity.

3. Purity

Knowing the truth about your real self, as we discussed previously, is an act of purity. "Purity" means unmixed, unadulterated, unalloyed. Therefore, purity implies oneness, doesn't it? One substance, without anything foreign mixed in. We routinely wash our bodies because we have a natural desire to remove anything foreign from our physical being. So, when we reject foreign, limited concepts about ourselves, we are expressing purity. We don't want our consciousness to hold "poisons" and foreign impurities such as anger, hurt, frustration, and other negatives, because they may take form as disease, including high blood pressure, heart attacks, and migraines.

If our Real Selves know only love and health, where do hate, illness, greed, lust, revenge, and all other negatives come from?

The answer is this: Negative concepts are not ideas at all; they are the absence of an idea, the unreal shadows of something real. When you see a shadow on the ground, you are not fooled into thinking it has substance. However, you do know there is something of real substance nearby that is casting the shadow. That is, the shadow tells you that something real is at hand. Can a shadow of yourself exist without you?

Here, then, is some good news: Negative ideas are substantially unreal, like shadows. When you experience them, they are only pointing to a real idea you are not expressing.

This means there is nothing standing in the way of your purity. Truly, there is only one reality, and you can make it your business to express it. You can fill the void of your negatives or anyone else's by forming the positive idea.

Take greed, for example, clearly a negative condition that creates all kinds of harm. Greed is the absence of the knowledge that you have the power to create all that you need out of your own ideas. Greed is the absence of the knowledge that you are complete and whole. If you truly *know* that you can have what you think, that you can have all you need, that you are complete and whole, you do not feel greed.

Hate is the absence of love. Does that sound too simplistic? That thing you hate so much—isn't it true that you hate it precisely because it falls so short of what you love? "I hate him" means "I love certain qualities he does not express." But because you know that hating will only reinforce and perpetuate the negative condition, fill this negative void with loving energy that will re-create the picture.

Fear is the absence of power. Fill this void by knowing who you are in Truth.

Continue for yourself, now. Ask, What idea is lacking when I feel sorrow? when I feel shy? when I feel anger? when I feel jealous? Go down your personal list and fill these voids with the pure ideas belonging to your Real Self.

Doesn't a healthy immune system operate on the principle of constantly distinguishing between self and not-self, and then eliminating what is not-self? Your mental immune system is your mental purity, the constant attention you give to which thoughts are Self (the Silent Master) and which are not-Self (negative and limited). When you express purity, you express the pure power and knowing of your Silent Master. You express your Real Self!

Purity leads to Love.

4. Love

Before you can express love, you must find love. You must know love within yourself before you can express it. You must love yourself before you can give it to another.

When you recognize or experience the *truth* about yourself you automatically feel love, because love is a quality of your true consciousness and true ideas.

Remember what we said of your Silent Master Consciousness:

VI

Your Silent Master expresses completeness, fulfillment, harmony, peace, joy, and Love, *and imparts these qualities to everything It creates.*

Thus, when you express *purity*—which is the truth about yourself, your Silent Master Consciousness—you feel a love for yourself that is expressed by self-respect, self-esteem, and self-confidence.

Love, and all the feelings of love, come with recognizing what is true about you and everything around you.

Experiencing gratitude is a simple way to connect with the love imparted to you and every idea in the universe. The direct experience of the consciousness of love is gratitude. Gratitude is the *process* of recognizing what is true. Gratitude is an act of awareness. Without awareness, there is no recognition of anything and, therefore, no love of anything.

I'll give you a small example of what I mean. Once I was driving west along the highway into a magnificent sun-

set. The entire sky was seemingly on fire with flames amazingly bright, burning colors: purple, orange, red, yellow,
blue, pink. I'd never seen so many colors in one place. Finding my vision restricted by the car windows, I pulled over
and got out so I could have a full view of this incredible
sunset. After a few moments I began to notice cars rushing
by. Some were filled with people talking to each other, in
another a man was using his car phone, in another someone
was trying to read a paper while keeping one eye on the
road. I was puzzled because not everyone was aware of the
magnificent sight in front of them. Most people seemed dis-
tracted in one way or another.

I was reminded of the power of gratitude. The feelings
I experienced with the sunset—the great peace, joy, appreciation, and *love* that welled up—seemed to exist only for
me at that moment. Of course, this sunset offered the opportunity for wonderful feelings to everyone else driving on
this road as well, but only those who were willing to acknowledge the sunset, to make a conscious recognition of its
presence, would feel the impact of its beauty. That is gratitude. Gratitude is the act of recognizing an idea or a quality;
and when you do so, you identify with it.

Thus, when you identify with a true idea through your
gratitude, you feel the force of the love it contains. Feeling
this love, you send it out again as greater, expanding gratitude. Then before you know it, your love is growing to ap-
preciate more and more of the world around you—people,
wildlife, nature, events. Ultimately, your consciousness becomes love, which you feel and express and which comes
back to you everywhere in every way, as beauty, harmony,
and peace.

So it is, when you express gratitude, you connect with
the Universal Love that is your Silent Master Consciousness.
You find love within yourself first, by recognizing the truth
of who you are. Then, as you express your purity, you auto-

matically begin to feel the love that is a part of all true ideas. You are loved, loving, lovely, and lovable. You are love.

Your awareness of love leads to loyalty.

5. Loyalty

Why does love lead to loyalty?

Love is its own reward. The wonderful feeling of love generated from expressing your real self naturally leads you to value your real self even more. Then, the more you value your real self, the more you love. This momentum of love is the essence of loyalty, so loyalty is the result of perpetuating, reinforcing, and expressing your real self by *loving* it.

And how do you love yourself? By being your real self. There is no greater way to love your real self than by being It. That is loyalty.

Here's an interesting thought you may not be aware of. The word "loyal" is derived from the Latin word *legalis*, which means "legal." Thus, loyal includes the meaning of legal, which means "bound by law." So, when you are loyal to your real self, when you are loyal to true and pure ideas about yourself, you invite the law of manifestation to operate and bring forth your real self. Loyalty is an act of acknowledging this law, an act of recognizing that whatever you are mentally loyal to is bound to take form.

Loyalty, then, is a lot like gratitude because they are both acts of recognizing or acknowledging an idea. Whatever you're loyal to, you recognize. Whatever you recognize, you think about. Whatever you think about, you manifest.

If you act with your body and mind as one, if you know the truth about yourself, if you express purity and love, you have done much to achieve your goal. It is at this point you must exercise loyalty to your cause so you bring your vision to completion, so you do not give up, turn back, regress, or undermine yourself.

Loyalty is a supreme act of love. Suppose you had a friend who gave you money when you were out of work, gave you a place to live when you had no home, saved your life when you were in trouble, told you to call anytime you needed help. Is this friend worthy of your loyalty? If one day this person asked you for your support, wouldn't you gladly give it, even if it involved some kind of sacrifice on your part? Most likely, you would do anything you could for this friend. Your loyalty would know no bounds.

If this is what you would do for a friend, how about your Self? What are you willing to do for it? Aren't you deserving of your own loyalty? How much loyalty are you willing to show your Silent Master, the infinite part of you constantly standing ready, like a friend, to give you everything?

Your Silent Master knows Its worth and value, knows It deserves all your love, energy, support—and loyalty. It knows It *is* truth, purity, and love—your truth, purity, and love. Thus, loyalty to your Silent Master is putting your real self forward with confidence, conviction, determination, purpose, power, and love. Show your loyalty! And as you do, you move as One with your Silent Master.

Loyalty leads to Sacrifice.

6. Sacrifice

When you have a goal that is a priority, and when you commit your total loyalty to this cause, you will undoubtedly make decisions about competing priorities in your life.

Remember the example of preparing to train for a marathon race? Attending every party in town could not be an equal priority to working out every day. One or the other must be chosen, the other sacrificed.

When your Silent Master gives you a desire, It will never ask you to sacrifice something you need. That is contrary to Its nature of love. When you find yourself at a crossroads and you must make a choice, look closely to see if the so-called sacrifice is really a loss. Usually, the things we give up to achieve a goal are no longer needed or are unworthy of keeping. If you give up laziness to keep your workout schedule, is that a loss? If you give up fear while learning something new, is that a loss? If you give up smoking to train for the race, is that a loss?

When we discussed increase and decrease with the yin-yang symbol, we said that every decrease (the black yin area) carries with it the seed of some new increase (the white dot in the black). Decrease is destined to turn into increase. So, even a real sacrifice is not ever really a loss. It is preparation for a new condition.

Many times it appears we are forced into a crossroads situation and we have to make a choice, a sacrifice. Sometimes, however, we can freely and willingly sacrifice certain states of mind to make room for the new.

The word "sacrifice" is derived from the Latin words *sacer*, meaning holy, and *facer*, meaning "to make." Sacrifice means "to make holy." So, when you sacrifice your weaknesses, fears, and limitations, you're actually loving yourself, making your self holy by expressing your truth and purity. This is a joyful, expanding process, no matter how painful it may appear on the surface.

Sacrifice leads to patience.

7. Patience

Let's assume you have a goal. You've acted with your body and mind as one, you have expressed truth, purity, love, loyalty, and you've sacrificed all mental and physical obstacles. Yet, the goal has yet to be realized. What's left?

Patience is the last step in this creative process. It is here that some impatient people may allow all their hard work to backslide.

One of nature's most beautiful symbols of patience is the transformation—the metamorphosis—of the caterpillar into a butterfly, when the outward picture of the caterpillar's "beingness" changes drastically from one form to another. Perhaps you have a situation that needs just such a radical transformation. If you desire to make a change as great as this, consider how the quality of patience is essential.

For a certain period, the caterpillar ingests food to enable it to grow to a certain point. This is a distinct period of time that cannot be rushed. When that point is reached, it then forms a cocoon in which it must wait for another period of time. A transformation occurs in the quiet cocoon that cannot be rushed or disturbed. Then at last, at the appointed time, a butterfly emerges, a different creature altogether from the caterpillar, who then reproduces so that the cycle begins all over again.

As the caterpillar goes through this transformation, there is something like trust going on, isn't there? Patience and trust. The laws of nature that enforce the caterpillar's miraculous transformation are absolute. All that's required in cooperating with the law is patience and trust.

The laws of manifestation that govern our being are just as absolute. We likewise must have the patience and trust to let them work.

True patience is *knowing* the truth and *expecting* the truth to manifest. This knowing and expecting is the process of *being* your Silent Master Consciousness. Thus, when you express this true patience, you think as your Silent Master thinks. You keep the power turned on as you wait knowingly for the manifestation to appear at its appointed time.

These seven principles of inner power are all intimately related to each other. You cannot fully practice one without including the others. That is, to practice Body and Mind as One, you need to practice Truth, Purity, Love, Loyalty, Sac-

75

rifice, and Patience, also. In reality, there's no such thing as, Today I'm working on purity. Each and every day, you work on all these principles.

As you make these qualities real in your everyday life, remember that what you are really practicing is your being-ness, your selfhood, your Silent Master. You're not asking yourself to be anything that's not real or not possible. Your Silent Master is your only true self. As you are joyfully and expectantly practicing these seven principles, you are becoming your Silent Master.

Unlike the caterpillar, usually we do not make our transformation in the darkness of a private space. Yet, ultimately, each of us is alone; each of us is a private individual. But we are alone together in a world of many people. Thus, our transformation is worked out in the world classroom. Much of our learning will be out in the open, composed of many small actions that will, step by step and moment by moment, create changes just as startling as the caterpillar's transformation. One painting is composed of thousands and thousands of brush strokes.

Our actions are guaranteed to affect others. Because we are not alone in this world, much of our learning about ourselves comes from our interaction with others. Our relationships are our teachers. We learn from each other.

There's a story I'm fond of that illustrates how we, as individuals, can make our own hell or heaven when we attempt to live together. This is hell: ten people are seated at a dining table. They have abundant food in front of them, but the chopsticks they're required to use are all three feet long. When they try to eat, they discover that the size of the chopsticks makes it impossible to feed themselves. They're all starving, quarreling, and fighting because they feel so thwarted and miserable.

This is heaven: ten people are at the same table with the same chopsticks. They are all happy, well fed, having a wonderful, peaceful time together. These people were un-concerned that they couldn't feed themselves with these long chopsticks. They used them to feed each other! The needs of every individual were met when they cooperated with each other, when they worked together.

Everyone and everything that comes into your aware-ness was drawn there by you. Therefore, as we go about our daily lives, we can have some grace; rather than regarding ourselves as victims, we can serenely see ourselves as the creators or co-creators of every moment. As individuals we create our private worlds, and collectively with other mem-bers of the planetary body we create our larger world. Regard every situation, then, private or global, as an opportunity to practice the truth of your being in your thought and actions, *your* being only. When you're being the best person you can be, don't be surprised if you find others transforming along with you!

CHAPTER 5

Your Silent Master in Action

PHYSICAL TRAINING IS LIFE TRAINING

Jung SuWon Physical Training

Up to this point, I have been concerned primarily with explaining the mental and spiritual concepts of Jung SuWon. But this art form also has a physical system, and learning the physical form of Jung SuWon is a practical and tangible way to put the spiritual principles of Jung SuWon into practice and to bring you into contact with your Silent Master Consciousness.

Your mind and body are one. Therefore, when you practice the Jung SuWon physical form along with the seven mental and spiritual principles, you develop your whole being, not your mind only, not your body only.

In this chapter, then, we will discuss several aspects of the physical training in Jung SuWon and the unique benefits available to you. Many of you who read this book will not have the opportunity to learn the physical aspects of Jung

SuWon. But you can still apply the principles in your physical life, in your physical activities.

Physical Training Is Overcoming Limitation

Certainly, increased physical strength and the knowledge of self-defense are desirable rewards of Jung SuWon martial art training; they reduce fear and weakness and build true confidence and self-esteem. Tae Kwon Do, Shotokan Karate, and Kung Fu are all similar in the origins of their basic forms. But the quality of physical training in Jung SuWon depends directly on the extent to which the spiritual training is applied. Learning the martial art moves and forms, learning how to spar effectively with an opponent, and demonstrating extraordinary physical feats (breaking bricks with your bare hand) require that you use all the principles of awareness, balance, visualization, commitment—all the rules of mental conduct—as well as the seven principles of inner power.

Training in the physical form of Jung SuWon requires that you focus all these ideas within the parameters of this structured art form and that you develop yourself and measure your progress in a disciplined manner. Your training, then, can be a feedback system, letting you know where you stand in taking control of your mind and body.

"He can do, she can do, why not me?"

This is a saying I teach students who are studying the physical form of Jung SuWon. This saying has several meanings that apply equally to mental, spiritual, and physical power.

First, on a physical level, it means that physical strength and the knowledge of self-defense derived from physical Jung SuWon training are available to both men and women alike. No one is limited by sex. Remember:

I

Your Silent Master is your
Real Self, your original Self.
It expresses Itself through
your thinking, through true
Ideas *and Thoughts in*
your mind . . .

"Strength" is one of the ideas expressed by your Silent Master Consciousness. It is part of your identity whether you are a man or a woman. Because strength is an idea, can the idea of strength be "stronger" in a man than in a woman? No. Ideas don't come in degrees of intensity. Ideas are just themselves, and they are the same in the minds of both men and women. Because I know this, and because I know strength is an idea belonging to my original self, I know I can manifest it; therefore, speaking for myself, I am not limited by my four-foot eleven-inch, ninety-pound body when defending against an attacker of much greater size and weight. I've proved it numerous times.

Second, the saying means that the spiritual principles of Jung SuWon are practical. When you use the principles, practice them, and apply them to the physical training, you discover that these principles are the foundation for your physical power. So, Jung SuWon is not just theoretical. It is to help you do whatever you need to do. "He can do, she can do, why not me?" And you can apply the principles to any situation in your life, not only in the school where you practice the physical martial art.

So, the foundation for your physical doing in Jung SuWon is the mental and spiritual training. Your physical strength is only as good as your mental strength. Powerful kicks and punches are worthless unless they are properly directed at an appropriate target, with the necessary mental focus. But all the physical strength in the world will not help if your mind is full of fear. Therefore, you must conquer fear and weakness within yourself before you can conquer a foe outside yourself. This is the purpose and essence of the Jung SuWon spiritual principles: to give you practical tools to free yourself from limiting, self-defeating states of mind. And it works!

"He can do, she can do, why not me?" A third meaning is that *you* have to have the mental attitude to do the work for yourself. He can do, she can do, why not *you*? Yes— those victories you've seen others attain? You can too! Why not you? Too many people shortchange themselves, discount themselves with too much fear and self-doubt. You have power! In reality, the only thing that separates you from your victory is work. If you are not mentally lazy, you have unlimited opportunity! This means *you* can *do*, if you are willing to take the necessary mental and physical steps and persist and persist until you win.

Physical Training Is Mental Warfare

In the first chapter I referred to the person seeking the Silent Master as a Jung SuWon Warrior for good reason. You are not a warrior only because you learn to physically fight. The seeker is a warrior also because the "not-self" traits you may have identified as "you" are not necessarily easy to relinquish. In fact, most of us experience a struggle of one degree or another every time we challenge a weakness in ourselves. It may take much time and persistence to rid yourself of unwanted characteristics. This can amount to a struggle that feels like warfare.

You may become keenly aware of your weaknesses and

negative thoughts and emotions as you train in a martial art because you're making greater demands on your body and asking yourself to perform in ways you previously considered impossible. But keep in mind, as we discussed in the section on Purity in chapter four, that your weaknesses are "shadows" of your real characteristics. The war against a shadow does not have to be waged with force. It's not sensible to fight against something that's insubstantial, is it?

Instead, the war can be won by gently embodying the real idea about yourself, whatever it may be at the time.

"Gently" doesn't mean "weakly," however. Gentleness is its own kind of force. Remember the fable about the contest between the Sun and the Wind? They each tested their power by attempting to make a man walking along a road take off his cloak. As the wind ripped and tore at the man with tremendous force, the man only drew the cloak tighter and tighter around him, until the Wind finally gave up and challenged the Sun. The Sun, however, showed no "force" at all; *gently* and *persistently*, it burned brighter and hotter, until the man released his hold on the cloak and took it off in the warmth of the day. This is the true nature of your conflict with yourself. Like the Sun, gently and persistently you must be who you are in truth.

Also during your warfare, remember what we discussed in the section on Truth in chapter four: To make your work easier, you must remain unimpressed with the evidence of your material senses. The material picture outside you is never the source of truth; it is a picture of what you've been believing to be true. Therefore, as a Jung SuWon warrior, you are not limited by any material evidence; you can change the picture when you change your thinking.

You are not limited.

Physical Training Is Observing Reality

Even if there were no martial arts systems in existence, we could still learn much about the valuable traits developed by these systems, like survival, self-defense, courage, discipline, and patience, just by watching nature. It's not by accident that many martial art forms incorporate the qualities of animals: the tiger, eagle, crane, bear, turtle, monkey. The original martial arts masters observed valuable traits in these animals, then imitated them to extend their fighting skills.

You may not be able to go directly to nature to learn basic truths and primal ideals embodied by nature's creatures; we do not live in nature the way people did thousands of years ago. So you, the modern warrior, may have to imitate others who have learned the way before you. However, you will still need to observe as much as the original warriors did. Your ability to observe is a powerful, essential weapon in self-defense.

How do you observe? By being *here, now* (as we discussed in Awareness in chapter three) so that you are undistracted by thoughts of the future or the past (which don't exist anyway). Remember we said that *now* is all there is; therefore, any blow coming to you, or any blow needed to strike at your opponent, can be known (or felt, or sensed) *now*. This foreknowledge (or ability to sense things) is the best offense and defense you can have and is the reward for being disciplined to live only in the NOW, the only reality. Thus, focusing on the present moment is truly observing reality, a skill cultivated in higher martial arts training. Certainly, to defeat an opponent, don't you need to be in the "right place at the right time"? Remember, the only time that can happen is *now*.

We also observe reality when we observe the symbols of reality. Isn't it true you often look at a photograph of a loved one when you can't be with him or her directly? The symbol takes the place of the person's presence.

Martial arts training cultivates a respect for and an acknowledging of the symbols of reality. In the do jang (the Korean word for "training hall") you will find attention given to symbols such as the uniform, the flags, and gestures of courtesy and respect; all are symbols of deep significance.

The Korean term for uniform is do-bok. Do means "way of life," and bok means "a spiritual protector or shield against the elements." Thus, the wearing of your uniform has great symbolic value. When you wear it, you also "wear" your commitment to follow the spiritual path leading to your Silent Master. Your commitment is assuredly your protection against the elements. The belt wrapped around your waist symbolizes the unity of spirit you share with others on the path, and its color proudly proclaims your level of achievement. When you honor your uniform, you honor your real self.

When you honor a country's flag, you honor the spirit of the nation. We could say that a flag is the face of the people, a symbol representing each individual who with many others form the spirit of the country. So, in the do jang, when you honor your country's flag, or another person, you honor your self and the self in others who create the nation.

And all gestures of courtesy and respect (such as bowing) honor the self in others in a most tangible and peaceful manner.

If you wish, you may regard your physical martial arts training as a comprehensive symbol of your life training. The mental and physical overcoming and strengthening that you demonstrate in the do jang represents the same overcoming in every other aspect of your life as well.

So, in martial arts training, we value symbols because it is a way to observe the real ideas the symbols represent.

Physical Training Is a Moving Meditation

Before we talk about a moving meditation, we should ask what meditation means.

Very simply, in spite of any religious connotations the word may have acquired, "meditate" simply means "to think about." The root of the word also held the meaning "to care about." So, in a meditation we think about what we care about.

However, because there are many different levels of thinking and of the quality of our thinking, there are different levels of meditation. Some kinds are more valuable, comprehensive, and far-reaching than others.

Generally, we meditate for a reason. We may wish to acquire some information outside our awareness; we may wish simply to relax, to feel the pleasure of our minds expanding; or we may wish to attain or visualize some desired result. Certainly meditation is a way to clear, cleanse, rejuvenate, open up, and expand our thinking.

No matter what your purpose for meditation, the reason for doing it is the same: to listen to your thoughts. On the most basic level, meditation is listening to the thoughts of your conscious or subconscious mind; on the most ideal level, meditation is listening to the thoughts of your Silent Master.

The process of meditation can be as informal as sitting quietly and listening to yourself. Or, you can adopt formal meditation postures and procedures to strive for deeper states of consciousness. Formal meditation as I teach it is a direct means for contacting your Silent Master.

Whether the meditation is informal or formal, there are always two steps. The first is to affirm to yourself that you and your Silent Master are One and to know and expect that the necessary information (or serenity, or clarity, or cleansing, or whatever) will manifest. Remember, your Silent Master Consciousness operates over and above both your conscious and subconscious mind; therefore, whatever your need, or whatever your purpose for the meditation, your Silent Master can effectively penetrate your conscious or subconscious mind, if necessary, to answer you appropriately.

The second step is to quiet your mind, so that all the clamoring thoughts and feelings are put aside. In this stillness, you can know and hear whatever you need.

Sometimes after meditating, you will get a "knowing" right away; however, you may have to repeat your meditation many times to bring about a desired result. Sometimes when you think you haven't received your answer, you will discover that your answer comes at the right time but not necessarily right away.

I refer to the physical practice of Jung SuWon as a moving meditation because the training requires you to focus your mind on specific ideas and qualities as you move. No movement in martial arts should be without direction or without thought; all movement should be focused and purposeful. Thus, this moving meditation involves concentration. The Latin roots of "concentrate" are *com*, meaning "together," and *centrum*, meaning "center." To concentrate means to "draw everything to a center." Thus, when you concentrate on a Jung SuWon movement, you are drawing your thoughts and actions to a central focus. Body and Mind as One!

Moving with your Body and Mind as One is a moving meditation.

You may ask, "If that's what a moving meditation is, what about when I'm balancing my checkbook, or cleaning house, or building a cabinet?" If so, you have grasped my meaning. Yes, these things, too, can be moving meditations if they are carried out in the spirit of Body and Mind as One. Any activity that brings you into a deeper communion with your real self is a moving meditation, whether it's playing the piano, walking in the woods, smelling flowers in the garden—whatever gives you this peaceful unity. In fact, the goal in Jung SuWon is to make our whole lives a moving meditation, a process where at all times we move as One with our Silent Master, thereby creating harmony, peace, right action, and everything that could be called love right where we are, right now! Jung SuWon physical training is really life training. We use the physical form as a training ground to grow and develop so that we master all areas of our lives.

CHAPTER 6

Meditation

COMMUNING WITH YOUR SILENT MASTER

In chapter five, I spoke of the physical training in Jung SuWon as a moving meditation. We saw that one of the most valuable goals of any meditation—moving or stationary—is to become one with your Silent Master Consciousness. Because your Silent Master is your personal focus for the Life Force of the Universe, through meditation you can seek to experience gifts of consciousness that exalt, uplift, energize, and harmonize your being, states of consciousness that are the experience of your true self. Thus, formal meditation can be one of the most satisfying, rewarding aspects of your life.

There is much to be said about the subject of meditation, and I will go into greater detail in another book. But for now, here is some introductory material so that you can begin meditation.

You meditate informally when you do just two things:

you consciously affirm your unity with your Silent Master, and you quiet your mind to listen. You can do these things anywhere, anytime.

Formal Meditation

There is much to be gained in formal meditation, where you adopt a specific posture, a procedure, and sometimes a specific environment to make a purposeful, dedicated, concentrated quest to experience your Silent Master.

There are many kinds of formal meditation. There are many postures and procedures, all having a unique purpose and meaning that enable you to strive for different outcomes in your meditations. Here is one example of a formal meditation you can easily try.

As you go through the steps, keep these two objectives in mind of knowing your unity with your Silent Master and quieting your mind.

1. Sit calmly on the floor or on a flat pillow. If you use a pillow, try to keep one especially for that purpose, one you do not use for anything else. If you need to purchase a pillow, silk or cotton ones are recommended.

2. Bend your right leg and place your foot under your left thigh.

3. Bend your left leg and lift the left foot onto your right thigh. If this hurts, don't force it; just do the best you can. Your legs should now be crossed with the right on the bottom and the left on top.

4. Bend your body forward, arch your back and then straighten up.

5. Place your right hand, palm facing up, gently on your lap.

6. Place your left hand, palm facing up, on your right hand and bring your thumbs together. The thumbs should be just barely touching, as if you were holding a sheet of paper between them.

7. Straighten your neck. Your head should be level, not up or down, and your ear lobes in line with your shoulders.

8. Close your eyes gently.

9. Close your mouth and place your tongue on the roof of your mouth.

10. Breathe in deeply through your nose, hold your breath as long as you can comfortably and then exhale slowly and softly. Your breathing should be gentle and quiet; someone sitting next to you should not be able to hear you breathe. Do this until your breathing is slow and gentle. You will probably notice your heart slows down as well.

11. Let any worries or concerns or clamoring thoughts and feelings flow away. Remember, initially your conscious mind feels uncomfortable when you ask it to suspend its habitual thinking processes (or more often, worrying processes). It wants to keep thinking and will try to do so. Just continue breathing, however, and refuse to pay attention to intrusive thoughts and feelings. Let them go, let them pass. If necessary, "tell them" you'll pay attention to them later, but not now (usually they go away when they have this "reassurance"). Right now, you want to strive for the most pristine purity and clarity of consciousness you can; and to do that, you must suspend your customary thinking processes. Eventually, you will feel your mind start to clear.

12. Now in this stillness, pose your question, your problem, your visualization, or whatever. *Ask.* Ask in whatever way feels right. Your Silent Master is listening.

13. Relax your mind, and determine now to let all thoughts flow to you freely. These thoughts will have a different feeling altogether than the clamoring ones you may have had in the beginning. These thoughts are messengers of one sort or another, responses swimming into your awareness as a result of your meditation. Do not become attached to any of them. Let them come and go as they will. Pay attention to them, but do not force yourself to analyze or think about them. You can analyze later, because your conscious mind is well equipped to do so.

Who am I?

The first question I asked you to pose at the beginning of this book was, Who am I?

My purpose in giving you the teachings of Jung SuWon has been to help you extend your vision of yourself.

It is at this point that you have enough tools to ask this question again. This time, however, I encourage you to pose this question to your Silent Master in formal meditation.

Who is more qualified to tell you who you are than your real self? Thus, the question Who am I?, when posed to your own Silent Master, is one of the simplest, yet one of the most profound meditations you can undertake. You are asking your real self to show you that It is You.

When you reach step 12 in the meditation procedure just given, ask, "Who am I?" This question is the complete meditation. You ask the question with all your feeling, lovingly and sincerely. You may repeat the question several times, slowly, and with full concentration. Then, you listen. . . . Listen until you have the knowing that you've listened long enough, even if you feel you haven't received any answer. You have; the answer will begin to manifest in many different ways for as long as you continue to repeat the meditation.

When you ask "Who am I?", you are subtly asking two questions: Who am I, the self that I know; and, Who is the "I" of the Silent Master? Of course, you are One, and this meditation helps bring about that realization (realization means to "make real").

Who am I? Remember, you are asking for something incredibly simple, really, something profoundly natural, something as close as your own being, yet something as infinite as the universe. Your Silent Master knows this question, and knows the answer. Now you, through your meditation, can also begin to know, to "make real" your unity with your Silent Master.

This meditation requires much repetition and patient listening. The understanding that results from it often doesn't happen all at once. The growing awareness can be so subtle that you don't realize you're getting it until you have it.

But this meditation is one that can be full of joyful surprises. It's definitely one that enlightens you in its own way, in its own time. But imagine the result! Imagine the joy of day by day growing into a fuller understanding of who you are—who you are, really, the power you really have.

It's this simple: your real self awaits your knowing. Let it come slowly, like the dawn, if it must.

For now, you, the Jung SuWon Warrior, can know:

You are One with the Universal Life Force.

The power that created galaxies, that formed oceans of

space, air, water—and consciousness—is the same power that flows through you and beats your heart and gives you consciousness!

As this power flows through you—you, as an individual focus of this power co-create with this Life Force, this universal Consciousness that knows only ideas expressing Universal Love!

And with this love, you create expressions of peace, harmony, balance, joy, beauty, fulfillment, and completeness. Then, wearing your clothing of material form, you look out upon these expressions with your physical senses and experience the challenge and the victory of those earthly creations.

And you say, "We are One."

Although you know that you are of this creation, you know you exist apart from it. You know that you are the Sun behind the sun, that your fire burns eternally behind everything that is known as time, and everything that is known as place, and everything that is known as this Universe.

And your fire is infinite Love, Awareness, Truth, Consciousness, which speaks to you and says,

"Before you are, I Am. And I Am You."

Epilogue

I offer the art of Jung SuWon to you knowing it will help
you find the serenity, love, freedom, and power that you
possess as an essential part of this universe. This is what you
are. It is your birthright. Claim it! You have the right to be
everything that you are, to know your power, to express and
create everything you desire in your heart.

I believe in your beauty, I respect your purpose in this
world, and I support your growing awareness of who you are
in truth. May you know the joy and excitement of creating
your life and all that you experience!

Grandmaster Tae Yun Kim

Acknowledgments

Today I am still a student as well as a Grandmaster. Every person who comes into my life teaches me. Each one is a unique individual with something special to give to the world. I thank God for the opportunity to help my students uncover their true strengths and abilities.

My special thanks go to Scott H. Salton and Michael B. Fell; senior instructors Thomas C. Saunders and Mark E. Amador; instructors Erika A. Sommers, Kristina S. Williams, and Chase S. Lang; and junior instructor Jacklyn Marie for putting forward their dedication, support, and commitment.

Finally, I want to thank all my students who put their energy together as *one universal mind, one strength, one power, and one healing force.* With the power of this unity, there are no obstacles we cannot overcome.

Thank you all.

About the Author

Grandmaster Tae Yun Kim is a world-renowned Ki energy master and one of the highest-ranked martial artists in the world.

Grandmaster Kim is the first female master of martial arts ever to come from Korea. She began at the age of seven, learning ancient, traditional methods of Ki energy development in the solitude of the mountains.

Grandmaster Kim is the CEO of Lighthouse, a successful computer company in Silicon Valley. She is also a dynamic lecturer and motivational speaker, addressing both business and personal success.

Most fundamental, however, Grandmaster Kim is a teacher. She works with people from all walks of life to help them overcome their difficulties and achieve their dreams.

Grandmaster Kim demonstrates the power of what she teaches in all areas of her life. At 52, she looks easily half her age and radiates beauty, health, serenity, compassion, and a zest for life.

OTHER RESOURCES
BY GRANDMASTER TAE YUN KIM

$10.95 **The Silent Master Book** — By following the Silent Master within, you can overcome any obstacle and rise above limitation. Each chapter outlines a different aspect of self-discovery and offers a specific lesson designed to put the concepts into action.

$14.95 **Secrets to Managing Your Energy: The Ki to Life** — Grandmaster Kim explains ki energy in terms of your environment, your relationships with others, your health, and your ability to create the life you've always wanted.

$29.90 **Seven Steps to Inner Power Workbook and Companion Book** — Improve your career, relationships, and health. Learn how to take charge of your life by setting goals and following through with the exercises and self-assessments.

$24.95 **Seven Steps to Inner Power Book on Tape** — You can read *Seven Steps to Inner Power* or listen to it! Grandmaster Kim speaks "between the lines" to add some extra surprises.

$12.95 **Whisper to Your Soul Audio** — Soothing and uplifting flute music played by Grandmaster Tae Yun Kim within the *Seven Steps to Inner Power Book on Tape*. Designed to relax the body, calm the mind, and free the spirit.

$12.95 **New Dimensions Audio** — A radio talk show broadcast world-wide on the New Dimensions radio show. A dynamic one-hour seminar with Grandmaster Tae Yun Kim on the topic of rising above your environment and the *Seven Steps to Inner Power*.

$29.95 **Seven Steps to Inner Power Video – Shim Gong** — Grandmaster Kim demonstrates *The Seven Steps to Inner Power* in this inspiring and action-packed video. Includes interviews of students who have used these principles to achieve outstanding results on the training floor and in their lives.

$29.95 **Reaching Beyond the Ordinary Video – Nae Gong** — Grandmaster Kim demonstrates five ways of thinking that will improve your physical performance. This is the groundwork for the Seven Steps to Inner Power, presented in a video full of practical philosophy and spectacular action.

$29.95   *The Power of Forms Video – Hyung* — This 60 minute video includes the most common Korean hard forms and traditional weapon forms as well as many soft forms rarely seen before.

$39.95   *Ki Rhythms Video* — This video takes you through step by step energy forms that help to reduce stress, help you focus on your goals, overcome obstacles and increase your energy.

$49.95   *Ki Energy, Set of 6 Audio Tapes* — This meditation series is a collection of beautiful music sung by Grandmaster Kim. Designed to recharge your energy while meditating, working at a desk, preparing a meal, driving a car, relaxing, or before you go to sleep.

$12.95   *Be Free Audio* — Virtually everyone has something that prevents them from being their best. Whether it's a lack of confidence, fear, stress, anger, jealousy, or another negative emotion, we must learn to let go and learn to Be Free.

$12.95   *Rising Above Audio* — Listen to the sounds of nature as Grandmaster Kim takes you through an inspiring meditation exercise designed to relieve stress and develop motivation.

$12.95   *Be An Original Audio* — Follow Grandmaster Kim as she leads you through the process of eliminating self-doubt and lack of confidence. Develop a greater feeling of self-worth. Yes you can do it!

$12.95   *Ocean Magic Audio* — Grandmaster Kim uses the power of the ocean along with a centuries-old meditation technique to produce an extremely relaxing and revitalizing mental state you can experience time and time again.

$12.95   *Grandmaster's Song Audio* — An instrumental music track inspired by Grandmaster Kim that is designed to release anxiety, relieve stress, and enhance clear thinking.

For more information, write to:

NorthStar
119 Minnis Circle, Milpitas, CA 95035
1-800-565-8713, Fax (408) 942-3307
www.gonorthstar.com

New World Library is dedicated to
publishing books and cassettes that inspire
and challenge us to improve the quality
of our lives and our world.

Our books and tapes are available
in bookstores everywhere.
For a catalog of our complete library
of fine books and cassettes, contact:

New World Library
14 Pamaron Way
Novato, CA 94949

Phone: (415) 884-2100
Fax: (415) 884-2199
Or call toll-free (800) 972-6657
Catalog requests: Ext. 900
Ordering: Ext. 902

E-mail: escort@nwlib.com
http://www.nwlib.com